CONFIDENT KIDS®

Guides for
Growing a
Healthy
Family

To Pastor Lee (Eliason), my teacher, counselor, mentor, and
friend,
whose wisdom and kindness guided me
through the long hard journey
of opening myself up to feel *all* my feelings.
Thank you for walking with me
through some of the most difficult moments
of my life.

Books in the
"Guides for Growing a Healthy Family" Series

I Always, Always Have Choices
All My Feelings Are Okay

Future books planned on these topics:

Family Communication Skills
Handling Significant Changes
Characteristics of a Healthy Family
Self-Esteem

All My Feelings Are Okay

LINDA KONDRACKI

Fleming H. Revell
A Division of Baker Book House Co
Grand Rapids, Michigan 49516

Scripture not otherwise identified is from the
New International Version,
copyright 1973, 1978, 1984 by
International Bible Society.
Used by permission of Zondervan Publishing House

Scripture identified ICB is from the
International Children's Bible, New Century Version,
copyright © 1986 by
Sweet Publishing, Fort Worth, Texas.
Used by permission.

The quote by David Norton in the introduction
is used with permission of David Norton
and David C. Cook Publishing Company.
It appeared in Tim Hansel's
Through the Wilderness of Loneliness.

Art direction and series design by Joy Chu
Production layout by Ellen Flaster
Illustrations by Cat Bowman Smith
Initial caps and logo on Read-Along Pages by Rita Pocock

Library of Congress Cataloging-in-Publication Data
Kondracki, Linda.
All my feelings are OK / Linda Kondracki.
p. cm. – (Guides for growing a healthy family)
ISBN 0-8007-5441-7
1. Emotions in children.
2. Expression in children.
3. Emotions–Religious aspects–Christianity
4. Child rearing–Religious aspects–Christianity
5. Children–Religious life
6. Child rearing
I. Title. II Series: Kondracki, Linda. BF723.E6K66 1993
649'. 7-dc20   92-41974

Copyright © 1993 by The Recovery Partnership
Published by Fleming H. Revell, a division of Baker Book House Company,
Box 6287, Grand Rapids, Michigan 49516-6287
Printed in the United States of America

C O N T E N T S

About the "Guides for Growing a Healthy Family" Series

The "Guides for Growing a Healthy Family" series is a collection of innovative programs written especially for parents of elementary-age children (although—with a little ingenuity—they can be adapted to include preschoolers and teenaged members of a family). Each book combines stories, discussion topics, and group activities that serve as a practical resource for teaching all family members a set of skills they need to have productive and emotionally healthy lives. For example, the first book introduced a guide for making wise choices; this one focuses on identifying feelings and expressing them in healthy ways. Future topics to be considered are family communication skills, characteristics of a healthy family, handling significant changes (grief), and self-esteem.

However, there is no particular order to the series. Parents are invited to start with any one book of their choice and proceed through the series in whatever sequence seems to best suit their family situation.

Goals
of the Series

1. **A "next step" resource to parents in recovery.** Many parents are still struggling with destructive behavior patterns they learned in childhood. Recovery groups, "inner child" workshops, and individual or family therapy sessions are helping millions of adults replace those patterns with new and healthier ways of living. Nevertheless, parents in such support programs often discover that their individual recovery journeys are not adequately preparing them to parent their own children. It is our natural instinct to repeat the patterns we saw in our family of origin, yet many people in recovery typically grew up in dysfunctional homes where the models of parenting were, at best, inadequate. Most recovery agendas do not directly address how parents can translate what they are learning about themselves into the skills needed to raise emotionally healthy children. The family guides can help parents in recovery take this next step.

2. **A tool parents can use to teach healthy living skills to their children.** Good parenting is mainly about teaching children sound values and behavior patterns that reflect their responsibility to themselves and others. Even parents who are quite clear on the values may be confused about what the related skills are, and how to go about teaching those skills in

the midst of the hectic, often fragmented family life so common in many modern American homes. The books in this series identify the key skills needed to grow a healthy family life and provide an easy-to-use, hands-on tool to enable all members to learn these important skills together.

3. **A means to build family connectedness.** A common problem for families today is a loss of a sense of solidarity. Here again, busy schedules and a variety of social and economic factors make it increasingly difficult for families to create and maintain strong bonds of togetherness. The family guides help in this area by suggesting both occasions and agendas for meaningful times of family interaction. By spending quality time together, your family will not only be learning new skills but also building lifelong relationships.

Format of the Family Guides

All the chapters, or units, in the family guides contain three sections, each of which approaches a particular aspect of a life skill from a different angle.

1. **"Getting Ready"—Parents' Pages**
   This introductory section is for your own growth, and it should be thoroughly worked through before getting the family involved. You cannot teach a skill to your children until you are on the way to mastering it yourself or at the very least understand why it is important. These pages

invite you to examine your own attitudes and behavior patterns and prepare you to personalize the material so as to meet the unique needs of your own family. Included here are *teaching pages* (the main point of the chapter, written at an adult level); *reflection questions* that relate the principle to your own experiences; and a *biblical truth* that will connect you to God and His Word.

2. **"Talking Together"—Read-Along Pages**

The middle section translates the main idea of the chapter into language your children can understand. Reading these pages together and talking through the questions will communicate valuable information on life skills in a relaxed family setting. Included here are *teaching pages* (written at a child's level); a *short activity* that invites group discussion and participation; a *story* and related questions; and a *summary statement* that clearly states a principle and related it to God's Word.

3. **"Growing Together"—Family Activities**

This final section is perhaps the most important one of all. Doing one or more of the suggested activities not only reinforces the skills building but will also provide occasions for bonding as a family. Included here are a *biblical teaching* that connects the skill to God's Word by memorizing a Bible verse and/or sharing a short Bible study; *conversation starters* (a time for open communication); and *family night* activities through which everyone can enjoy a fun time together and learn valuable skills at the same time. There are instructions for a variety of things to do, including crafts, plays, family outings, and more.

How to
Use the Guides

Getting maximum benefit from the family guides will require planning and work on your part. Once you have chosen a book in this series, here is a suggested way to proceed:

1. **Familiarize yourself with the "Stages of Skill Development" (see Appendix A).** Always remember that learning new skills takes time and feels uncomfortable at first!

2. **Study the material in each chapter before presenting it to your family.** This means not only working through the Parents' Pages, but reading the other two sections as well. For example, understanding the Read-Along Pages and relating them to your own situation at home will prepare you for possible answers to the discussion questions.

3. **Work through the book systematically, preferably by dealing with one chapter each week.** Difficult as it may be to arrange, try to set aside a weekly time slot for family interaction, whether in the early evening or during the weekend. Mark it on the calendar and be sure all family members understand the importance of being there.

4. **Make advance preparations by gathering any items needed for family activities.** It will spoil everyone's fun if there is a last-minute search for supplies.

5. **Have fun together!** Perhaps the greatest benefit of using these guides comes when you can all learn to relax and enjoy just being together. As a parent, having realistic expectations increases the possibility that this will happen more and more frequently, as will your insistence on everyone's following the "Rules for Family Interaction" outlined in Appendix B.

Because the discussions and activities will not always happen as smoothly as they sound in this book, visible moments of growth may seem slow in appearing. In fact, there will be times when you think your kids are not learning a thing. But, even then, you will not be wasting your time, because you are accomplishing a great deal just by being together.

If you would like more information about starting a Confident Kids® Support Group program in your congregation or community, please write:

CONFIDENT KIDS®

℅ The Recovery Partnership
P.O. Box 11095
Whittier, CA 90603

I N T R O D U C T I O N

I have often marveled at how we humans so value the spiritual and cognitive aspects of our person while devaluing the emotional aspect—as if God, when He was creating human beings, only got two-thirds of it right.

David Norton

My friends in college used to say, "Linda, you're the most emotionally stable person we know!" At the time I remember responding with "thank you," but silently adding "I think." Even then, something about their words didn't sound right. It wasn't until many years later, at a particularly difficult time of my life, that I finally began to understand why. What my friends had seen in me and interpreted as stability was in reality a state of being emotionally *frozen*. The fact that I never showed anger or hurt or got wildly excited over anything was not because I was in control of my feelings but because I was unable to feel at all.

I have discovered over the years that my experience is not unique. Many of us grew up without ever learning the skills of accepting and dealing with all our feelings in healthy ways. Instead, in our formative years, we heard messages that denied us our feelings:

"You shouldn't feel that way!"
"What are you crying about? We'll get you another dog."
"Big boys don't cry." (Or, "Nice girls don't scream.")
"Stop making such a fuss!"

"The Bible says "don't be angry," and you can't act that way in this house!"

"Dad does *not* have a drinking problem. Don't you ever say that again!"

You can probably add similar messages of your own. The result of growing up with a steady diet of such negative statements is that we come to believe that if we feel bad, we are bad! So, we learn to avoid feeling bad in one or more of the following ways:

▸ By behaving in certain ways—don't cry; don't be angry; don't grieve; always smile and stay calm.

▸ By not talking about what's real—don't mention Dad's drinking; don't tell anyone about the way Uncle George touches you; keep quiet about your fears.

▸ By pretending you don't feel pain, so "there is nothing to deal with, thank you very much!"

The fact that God has created us to feel a wide range of emotions can seem like both a blessing and a curse. Along with the ability to feel deep love and pleasure and excitement, He has also given us the capacity to feel great pain and anger and loneliness. The point of difficulty comes when we try to ignore the uncompromising truth that *we cannot have one without the other!* When we try to cut ourselves off from emotions that make us uncomfortable, we are seriously hampering our ability to feel anything at all.

This book is about learning to open ourselves up to the whole range of feelings that God has placed within us, and developing the skills we need to handle those feelings positively.

A healthy family is a safe haven, a support system, and the primary classroom in which we learn how to identify and express our feelings. The family unit and each of its members will be strengthened to the degree that all feelings are explored, appreciated, and managed responsibly.

It is my prayer for every family that sharing the experience of welcoming and handling the marvelous variety of feelings that God has created will enrich the quality of your lives, both at home and beyond your front door. In the weeks ahead, I hope you and your children will relax and have a good time with the activities in this book, as you learn together that *all your feelings are okay!*

CHAPTER

ONE

I Need Every Feeling

GETTING READY

Feelings:
Friends or Foes?*

It was the first night of a new unit in our Confident Kids support-group program. Joey walked into the room, stood in front of his leader with his hands on his hips, and announced, "I shouldn't be here, 'cause I don't have any feelings. So I got nothin' to talk about!" For the entire eight weeks of the unit, Joey held tenaciously to his position that he had no feelings—except for one incident that captured his attention.

On the fifth evening, the kids were using puppets to role-play various hypothetical situations. When they got to the one that said, "Your parents just told you they are getting a divorce," Joey's hand shot up. "I want to do that one," he said. Taking a puppet in his hand, he continued, "*If* I had feelings, which of course I don't, but *if* I did, I'd feel angry." He paused for a moment and then added, "Because parents don't tell you when they're gonna get a divorce—they just leave!"

Joey was in second grade, and he had already discovered that life is full of feelings that are not fun to feel. His response was simply deciding not to feel them. What he was too young to understand, however, is that it is not possible to shut out only certain emotions. When we choose not to feel *some* feelings, we are actually cutting ourselves off from the ability to feel at all. The result? As Joey said, "I don't have any feelings. So I got nothin' to talk about!"

*Parents are urged to read "How to Use These Guides," Appendix A, and Appendix B for helpful directions to receive maximum benefit from this series.

Many of us grew up just like Joey. Somewhere along the way, we discovered that some feelings are not fun to feel, and we responded by finding ways not to feel them. In the process we cut ourselves off from one of the most important aspects of living a healthy life—the ability to feel all our feelings. Our first task, therefore, is to give ourselves and our children permission to feel *all* our feelings. Here are three simple steps to help us get started:

1. **Realize there are no good or bad feelings.** Most people instinctively believe that if a feeling feels good, it is good; if it feels bad, it is bad. If we are to feel all our feelings, we must come to see that feelings are neither good nor bad—they are simply an expression of what is happening inside of us.

   Changing the way we refer to feelings from "good" and "bad" to "comfortable" and "uncomfortable" (or "difficult") is a simple way to begin opening up to the whole range of feelings that God has placed within us. When we label certain feelings as "bad," we are really sending a message that tells us to get rid of them, for we were taught, and we teach our children, to stay away from or cleanse ourselves of bad things. On the other hand, saying that a feeling is "uncomfortable" or "difficult" invites us to find a way to deal with it. Uncomfortable experiences may not be fun, but handling them appropriately is a normal part of what healthy living is all about.

2. **Discover the purpose of each feeling.** Every feeling provides us with valuable information we must have to stay safe, meet our personal needs, and develop sound relationships. For instance:

   ▸ Fear warns us of danger and tells us to seek protection and comfort.

- ▶ Anger serves as a signal to let us know our own or someone else's rights are being violated. It is a safety valve that helps us release strong emotional pressure and generates the strength to handle whatever situation is before us.
- ▶ Loneliness tells us that our basic need for relationships and intimacy is not being met and motivates us to reach out to others.
- ▶ Pain lets us know that something significant has hurt us; it says we are in need of healing.
- ▶ Joy is an indication that our needs are being met.
- ▶ Pride tells us that we are doing something well, thereby affirming our sense of self-worth.

And so on. Each feeling we experience in life plays a part in keeping us in touch with our needs and whether or not they are being met. When we cut ourselves off from even one feeling, we shut down a significant source of information.

3. **Learn to name feelings accurately.** To effectively gather the information our feelings provide, we must be able to name what we are feeling at any given point in time. For instance, it is not helpful for me to say, "I feel awful"—that is too vague and undefined. However, saying "I feel lonely" *is* helpful—now I know that I am feeling "awful" because my relational needs are not being met. In response, I can find a way to reach out. In the same way, "I feel happy" is not very informative—it is also vague and undefined. But "I felt welcome and included at the neighborhood picnic today" helps me see that I have found a place to get the important need of "belonging" met.

Feelings are a tremendous gift that God has given us. Knowing that "All my feelings are okay" is the first step to living the emotionally healthy lives God intends for us.

For Reflection

1. In your family of origin, which feelings were "okay"? _____
   _____

   Which ones were not allowed? _____
   _____

2. What experiences can you remember that might have caused you to block out certain feelings?
   ☐ Parents' divorce
   ☐ Chemically dependent family member
   ☐ Emotional, physical, or sexual abuse
   ☐ Teasing in school for being too fat, tall, dumb, or _____
   ☐ Other: _____
   ☐ Other: _____

   What experiences have helped you open up to your feelings?
   ☐ Parents were open and allowed me to talk through all my feelings.
   ☐ Schoolteachers, youth sponsors, scout leaders, coaches, or other mentors took a special interest in me.
   ☐ Recovery groups, counseling, and other support systems helped me during my adult development.
   ☐ Other: _____

☐ Other: _____

3. Turn to the list of "feelings" words on pages 22-23. Read through the list slowly, paying attention to your emotional reaction to each one. Then read through the list once more, identifying the following:

Feelings you are comfortable feeling and expressing _____
Feelings that frighten you _____
Feelings you are unable to feel at all _____

Describe any patterns you see or insights you gained from doing this exercise. _____
_____
_____

Building On God's Word

Learning to feel all our feelings can be a frightening and painful experience. If you are struggling with this part of your life, remember that you do not have to face this journey alone. You can have the presence and power of God to guide you through it. Let this promise from God's Word give you hope and strength:

"Have I not commanded you? Be strong and courageous. Do not be terrified; do not be discouraged, for the Lord your God will be with you wherever you go." *Joshua 1:9*

TALKING · TOGETHER

What Are You Feeling Today?

Feelings can be hard to talk about. When someone asks, "What are you feeling today?" it's not always easy to answer. Feelings are something we don't think about very much because they are just part of our day-to-day lives. In fact, the only thing some people think about them is:

"There are good ones and bad ones—and I would rather not think about the bad ones!"

Actually, that question, "What are you feeling today?" is an important one for us to answer. Our feelings help us in many ways, and paying attention to them is part of living in a healthy way. Here are just a few things feelings do for us:

▶ **They give us pleasure.** Feeling happy or excited or proud or loved is an enjoyable part of life. It's hard to imagine what life would be like if nothing ever made us happy or we never felt loved by anyone or we never got excited the night before Christmas. It is such pleasant feelings that let us enjoy all the special moments in our lives. In the blank faces below, draw what each feeling looks like:

Happy   Excited   Loved   _____ _____ _____

(Add other feelings that give you pleasure)

11 ▶

▶ **They warn us when something is wrong.**
Feeling angry or frightened is often a signal
to us that something is wrong. For instance,
when we feel angry, it could be because
someone or something *has* hurt us. When we
feel frightened, it could be because someone
or something *could* hurt us. We can be safer
and take better care of ourselves if we pay
attention to such feelings and use them as a
signal to get help.

Draw these feelings:

Angry   Frightened   _____ _____ _____

(Add other feelings that warn you when something is wrong)

▶ **They help us get our needs met.** When we feel confused or lonely or sad, we are not getting something we need. For instance, if we are confused by something a teacher asks us to do, *we need more information.* If we are lonely, *we need a friend,* someone special to talk to or play with. By paying attention to such feelings we can find a way to get what we need.

Draw these feelings:

Confused   Lonely   Sad   _____   _____   _____

(Add other feelings that help you get your needs met)

As you can see, every feeling we have is important. It's not true that there are "good" feelings and "bad" feelings, but because *some* feelings are very hard to feel, we would rather *not* feel them. Although no one likes to feel angry or sad or lonely, those emotions have a purpose, and learning to feel them is a big part of having a safe and healthy life.

Here's a story about a boy who learned to pay attention to and talk about what he was feeling:

The Hurt Heart

Carol walked up to the door of Clyde's house and rang the doorbell. Clyde was her best friend in the whole world. She didn't exactly know why, but Carol guessed the main reason she liked Clyde so much was all the crazy stuff he did. One thing about good old Clyde—when you were with him, you never knew what was going to happen next!

"Hi, Carol," Clyde said as he opened the door and stepped aside so his friend could come in.

"Hi, big guy," Carol greeted him as she stepped inside the house. "Wanna ride bikes over to. . . ." She stopped in mid-sentence, noticing Clyde's bandaged hand and the pained look on his face. "Hey, what happened?"

"Nothin'," Clyde said softly, looking away from Carol.

"Waddaya mean, nothin'? You got a big bandage on your hand!" Suddenly, Carol brightened, clapped her hands together, and

"I can hardly wait to hear! What happened this time?"

"It was just a little accident, that's all," Clyde responded, still not looking at his friend.

"Oh, boy! Your accidents are exciting! Tell me more!"

"Come on, Carol, lay off. It was nothin'. Okay?" Clyde started to walk back toward the kitchen, but Carol was right behind him, determined not to give up.

"No way! I'm not leaving you alone till you tell me what happened!" she insisted.

Knowing just how persistent Carol could be, Clyde turned and faced her. "I was just eating some soup, that's all."

"Eating soup? How can you hurt your hand eating soup?"

"Well, I dropped my spoon on the floor."

"Yeah, so?" Carol looked puzzled.

"When I went to pick it up, I bumped into the table."

Carol giggled, beginning to get the picture. "*That* sounds like the good old Clyde I know and love! Then what happened?"

Clyde sighed, realizing he'd passed the point

of no return. Carol would never give up until she heard the whole story, and he knew what that would mean. He continued, "When I bumped the table, the bowl started to fall, and I tried to catch it. Only I missed and stuck my hand right into the boiling-hot soup that Mom had just poured from the pot on the stove."

Laughing hysterically, Carol said, "Boy, Clyde! You do more clumsy stuff than anyone I know!" Then, although she had thought this was a great moment to be enjoyed, Carol noticed that Clyde looked sad and hurt. "Ah," she said awkwardly, "I guess it really hurt, though, huh?"

"Not as much as my heart hurts right now," Clyde said softly.

"Your *heart?* Are you okay? Gosh, Clyde, you're not having a heart attack, too, are you?"

"Of course not! I don't mean my *real* heart, I mean my 'feelings' heart. Look, Carol, I know I do clumsy stuff a lot, and sometimes it is pretty funny. . . ."

"Yeah," Carol interrupted, once again enjoying herself. "Like the time you tripped in the school lunch line and spilled your meat loaf and carrots all over Mr. Roberts! Boy, the look on his face!"

"That's just what I mean, Carol. Everyone laughed, but I felt stupid—and like I wanted to die! I guess what I'm trying to say is that the hurt I feel on the inside when everyone laughs at me is worse than any hurt on the outside. Even this burn doesn't hurt as much as my heart does when you make fun of me."

Finally, Carol began to understand at least a little of what her friend was feeling. "Wow, I never thought about it like that. When I get hurt on the inside, I try to think about somethin' else so it doesn't hurt so much, but that doesn't always work. Hey, wouldn't it be great if we had somethin' like a bandage for our inside hurts? You know, kinda like that one you have on your hand?"

Clyde just looked at Carol and shook his head. But he smiled to himself as he turned and continued his journey to the kitchen.

What Do You Think?

▶ Name a time your heart hurt like Clyde's did.

▶ Do you agree that feeling hurt on the inside can be worse than feeling hurt on the outside?

▶ Besides feeling hurt, what other kinds of feelings do we feel on the inside?

Remember...

**You need *all* your feelings
to live a healthy life.**

Sometimes feeling all our feelings can be scary. But, you don't have to face them alone! Here's a promise from the Bible that can help you during those times.

"Have I not commanded you? Be strong and courageous. Do not be terrified; do not be discouraged, for the Lord your God will be with you wherever you go." *Joshua 1:9*

Growing Together

BUILDING ON GOD'S WORD

Joshua 1:9 Posters. Give everyone paper and markers or crayons. Then read Joshua 1:9 together and ask all family members to make a poster illustrating times they have felt terrified and/or discouraged. (If they can't think of real experiences, they can make a poster of things that would terrify or discourage them.) When all have finished, ask family members to talk about their posters.

End your sharing time with a simple prayer thanking God for His promise to be with us always. Encourage all family members to participate. Anyone who needs it can use the following prayer, filling in specific feelings and experiences from the posters:

> Dear God,
> Thank You for always being with me, even when I feel
> _____ because _____.
> Amen.

CONVERSATION STARTERS

Play Feelings Charades. Family members can increase their "feelings" vocabulary by acting out certain words. Make a list of feelings to use for the game (refer to the words on pages 22-23 for possibilities). Write the words you selected on individual slips of paper and place them in a basket or other container. To play, everyone takes a turn choosing a slip from the container and acting it out for the rest of the family. When the feeling has been correctly identified, ask for volunteers to tell about a time they have experienced that feeling or something they think might cause them to feel it.

FAMILY NIGHT ACTIVITIES

Make Feelings Wheels. Learning to name our feelings accurately takes practice. Using Feelings Wheels to check in with each other on a daily basis can help. You will need a dinner-sized paper plate, a 3" x 5" card, and a small brad for each family member, plus a variety of markers, crayons, stickers, and other items everyone will enjoy using to decorate the wheels.

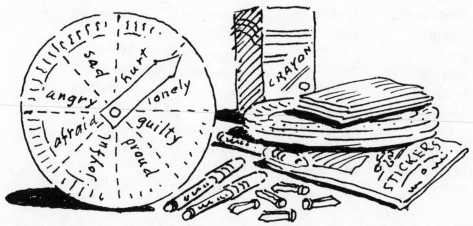

Growing Together

Have family members divide their plates into eight sections and write the following "feelings" words in them: *sad, angry, afraid, joyful, proud, guilty, lonely,* and *hurt.* (You can do this ahead of time for young children.) Let everyone color and decorate his or her wheel. Then cut pointers out of the file cards, write family members' names on them, and attach them to the center of the plates, using the small brad.

Display the Feelings Wheels where they can be easily seen and use them to check in with each other regularly. For instance, you might have a time after dinner when family members turn the pointers on their wheels to indicate what they are feeling at that time. Give everyone a chance to share why that selection was made, honoring anyone's choice to "pass."

LIST OF "FEELINGS" WORDS

*angry	beaten	disappointed	eager
abandoned	broken	depressed	evaluated
accepted	bad	dominated	
anxious		desperate	***fearful**
alienated	closed	devastated	favored
apathetic	comfortable	dear	friendless
appreciated	cared for		failure
	curious	embarrassed	funny
beautiful	creative	excited	fat
bewildered	cautious	envious	
brave		energized	***guilty**

(*indicates a **primary feeling**)

gutsy	kind	pressured	torn
grateful	kid-like	proud	task-oriented
genuine	kneaded	possessive	touchy
grief-struck		passive	
generous	*lonely	persecuted	useless
good	*loved	peaceful	ugly
	loyal		unappreciated
*hurt	lacking	quiet	up-tight
hateful	loud		underachieving
hurried	lost	rejected	understanding
hopeful		reaching out	
happy	misunderstood	real	vivacious
harassed	manipulative	repulsive	vict.imized
	manipulated	rapturous	vindictive
in control	misplaced	restrained	vital
insecure	melancholy		
insensitive	masked	*sad	weary
incompetent		*shamed	wistful
independent	needy	supported	weepy
isolated	needed	supportive	wide-eyed
inhibited	negative	suspicious	wasted
	nosy	silly	winning
*joyful	nonexistent	stubborn	
jumpy		satisfied	x-rayed
jealous	outsider	soft	
judgmental	out of control		youthful
jagged	optimistic	terrified	yearning
justified	open	timid	
	overcontrolled	threatened	zany
			zealous

23 ▶

CHAPTER

TWO

No
Stuffing
Please

GETTING READY

Doing
It My Way

Have you ever heard (or made) comments like these?

"Poor Josephine! Imagine having your husband walk out on you after twenty-five years of marriage! But she's taking it very well. She told me 'he's not worth crying over,' and 'life goes on.' Of course, I'm not surprised—nothing ever seems to bother her, especially in a crisis."

"I don't know why Joe stays in that job. His boss humiliates him all the time, but he just smiles and takes it. Of course, with four kids at home, he can't risk being out of work."

"I'm so sorry about your father, Billy. But, remember, you have to be strong for your mother. You're the man of the house now!"

Each of these scenes reflects a denial of one of our most basic needs: to feel and openly express the emotional responses we have to our life situations. As much as we may wish it to be true, it is not possible to handle our feelings by ignoring them or pretending they don't exist. Here are three important points to remember about expressing our feelings:

1. **Feelings will be expressed eventually.** A fundamental truth of emotional health is this: **Unexpressed feelings do**

not go away—they simply get stuffed down inside until they find their own way to get out.

Feelings are a source of energy. As we discovered in the first chapter, when that energy is used properly it helps us live in a healthy way. However, denying the energy does not diffuse it. It's like steam rising from a boiling liquid. Putting a lid on the pot, so we cannot see the steam, does not get rid of it. Eventually, the pressure will be released—with or without our help.

The same is true with our emotional energy. All our feelings will be expressed eventually, in one way or another. Unless we find healthy ways to do it, they will show up in one or more of the following ways:

▶ Stress-related illnesses, such as ulcers or headaches
▶ Becoming easily irritable and angry without knowing why
▶ Overreacting to certain people or experiences for no apparent reason

We can avoid these things by finding more constructive outlets for our emotional energy.

2. **Feelings can be expressed in many different ways.** Although we all feel the same feelings, people have many different ways of expressing them. Look carefully at the following list of items:

▶ box of tissues
▶ pair of running shoes
▶ telephone
▶ notebook and pen
▶ drawing paper and paints or crayons

- ▶ stationery and envelopes
- ▶ pillow
- ▶ punching bag

This list suggests a wide variety of healthy ways to express our feelings. Our task as parents is twofold: find the ways that work best for *us*, and to help our children find ways that work for *them*.

As we were talking about this in one of our Confident Kids parents' groups, I noticed one mom who was deep in thought. "I've been thinking about my son," she said finally. "You know, he's a very active and athletic little boy. But whenever we get into a conflict, which we do on a regular basis, and he gets angry, I send him to his room and make him lie on his bed until he calms down. I've never felt like that worked very well, but I didn't know what else to do. Maybe I should tell him to put his sneakers on and go run around the block a few times instead of sending him to his room!"

The next week, this mom returned to the group with a big smile on her face. She told us, "When my son and I got into a conflict this week, I told him to go out and run around the block a few times. He went out and I lay down on *my* bed for a few minutes. You know, when he came back inside, we were both calmer—and we actually sat down and talked through our conflict. I guess he needs to express *his* feelings his way, not mine!"

3. **We need to observe the rule of expressing feelings.**
Finding our own way to express our feelings does not give us or our children permission to indulge in a feelings "free-for-all."

We can avoid that by observing one simple rule:

It is okay to express your feelings anyway you choose, except you may *not* be destructive to yourself, others, or property.

For example:

▶ It's okay to go to your room and be alone for a while. It's *not* okay to cut yourself off entirely from the people who care about you (that's destructive to yourself).

▶ It's okay to tell your friend you were hurt that she told your secret to someone. It's *not* okay to spread gossip about her to get even (that's destructive to others).

▶ It's okay to punch out your pillow when you're angry. It's *not* okay to throw your truck through the TV screen (that's destructive to property).

Allowing ourselves and our children to feel and openly express all our feelings will enrich both our personal and family lives— guaranteed!

F o r   R e f l e c t i o n

1. In your family of origin, how did family members express "pleasant" emotions, such as feeling happy, excited, proud, silly?

☐ Everyone joined in, and we had a family celebration.

☐ The kids could act happy and silly, but the parents did not participate.

☐ These feelings were considered self-indulgent, and we were not allowed to express them openly.

☐ Other: _____

☐ Other: _____

2. What happened when someone was angry, sad, scared?

☐ We were told, "There's nothing to be angry [sad, scared] about."

☐ We were sent to our rooms until we could calm down and act "appropriately."

☐ We were allowed to express our feelings openly.

☐ Other: _____

☐ Other: _____

3. Write down any feelings you currently have trouble expressing openly (ones you stuff inside). _____

_____

Set a goal to express one of those feelings in a healthier way this week.

Feeling: _____

I will express this feeling by: _____

Building On
God's Word

The Book of Psalms is actually a collection of poems, hymns, and prayers written to God. Within them, can be found an honest expression of every feeling that exists. Read the Psalms listed below and identify what feeling is being poured out to God:

Psalm 22—Feeling: _____

Psalm 61—Feeling: _____

Psalm 66—Feeling: _____

Psalm 121—Feeling: _____

What are you feeling today? Write a psalm or prayer to God, honestly pouring out that feeling to Him.

Let Your Feelings Out!

Did you know that every human being who lives anywhere in the whole world feels exactly the same feelings you do? And that all people who have ever lived from the very beginning of time have had those same feelings? When something good happens, you feel happy. When you are with someone who takes care of you and is kind, you feel loved. When you do something wrong, you feel guilty. When you lose something

31 ▶

or someone you love, you feel grief and are sad. Those feelings are the same for all of us.

Even though our feelings may be the same as someone else's, there are many different ways to express them. When feelings are fun to feel, it's easy to let them out. When they make us feel uncomfortable, however, we may try to find ways *not* to feel them. But whether they are fun or difficult to experience, all our feelings need to be released in healthy ways. Here are three things about expressing feelings you need to know:

1. **Pretending you are not feeling something does not make the feeling go away.** We call that stuffing the feeling inside, and when we do that, the feeling will struggle to get out, whether we want it to or not. Have you ever had a time when you were so excited you felt like you were going to burst if you didn't tell someone about it? That's what it's like to have a feeling inside struggling to come out. By telling someone about how we feel, we are letting that feeling out, or expressing it.

   What happens when we try to stuff our feelings inside and never let them out? They find a way to get out all by themselves, and we might not like how or when that happens. Left on their own, feelings can come out by:

▸ Making us sick, like giving us headaches or stomachaches or chills
▸ Giving us nightmares
▸ Making us nervous or anxious about every little thing that happens

A much better way is to learn to express our feelings in healthy ways, rather than stuffing them inside.

2. **You can find your own way of expressing your feelings.** There are lots of ways to get your feelings out. Look at each item below and write one idea of how it can help you express your feelings.

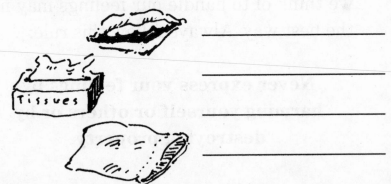

You can experiment with lots of different ways of expressing your feelings until you find the ones that work best for you.

3. **You may express your feelings in any way that works for you, as long you follow one simple rule.** Sometimes the first way we think of to handle our feelings may not be the best way. Always follow this rule:

> **Never express your feelings by harming yourself or others or by destroying property.**

For instance:

▶ It's okay to be angry if your little sister broke your model airplane. It's not okay to hit her in response. Punch your pillow instead.

▶ It's okay to feel hurt if your best friend tells your secret. It's not okay to tell lies about her to get even. Instead, try writing a letter to her, telling her how you feel.

Expressing your feelings by being destructive to yourself, others, or property will only make things worse. Don't do it—you can find better ways to let your feelings out!

Here's a story about a girl who discovered what happens when we try to keep our feelings inside:

The Letter

Clara stood next to her desk, looking as if an alien from outer space had just taken over her body.

"Hey, Clar, let's go," her best friend, Jennifer, called over her shoulder. "It's recess. Aren't you comin'?"

Slowly returning to earth, Clara smiled widely and bounded toward her friend. "You bet! We gotta hurry or we'll miss gettin' a turn on the swings!"

On the way outside, Jennifer looked at her friend with concern. "Clara, are you okay? I know it really hurt when your dad moved out."

"I'm fine, really!" Clara answered with a smile that was a little too big. "Yeah, it was hard at first when Dad left. But, hey! Who cares? I still have a life, you know. Come on, let's grab that swing over there before Sara Jane and her crew get it!"

After school, Clara asked her mom if it would be all right to have a sleep-over party for her birthday, which was still two more weeks away. Mom said she thought it would be okay. "Great!" Clara shouted as she took off for the phone to call Jennifer. "I hope she's home, I can hardly wait to tell her," she said to herself as the phone rang one, two, three times.

"Hello?" Jennifer was not only home, but had answered the phone.

"Jen, guess what? My mom said I can have a sleep-over for my birthday party in two weeks! Won't that be great? Who else should we invite, do you think? Of course, we won't invite Sara Jane or any of her crowd, but other than them, who should we ask?"

There was a long pause on the other end of the phone. Then Jennifer said, "Don't you remember? My family's taking a spring vacation this year. I won't be here for your birthday. I told you that a long time ago. I guess you just forgot."

Clara felt as if the worst thing that could possibly happen in the whole world had just happened. Her very best friend would not be at her birthday party. "What do you mean? You *have* to be there! You're my best friend! I can't have a birthday party without you!"

"Clara, I'm sorry! But I can't stay home from our vacation just to go to your birthday party. You'll have fun anyway. You have lots of friends!"

Clara slammed the phone down without saying good-bye and ran into the kitchen where her mother was doing the dishes. "Mom," she screamed at the very top of her voice, "the worst thing in the whole world just happened! I think I'm going to *die!*" Clara started prancing around the kitchen like a cat on a hot sidewalk, not knowing where to go or what to do. Suddenly, she picked up a glass and threw it against the wall. "I hate Jennifer!" she yelled.

Clara's mom turned off the water and stared at her daughter. "Clar, what's wrong? What happened?" She expected to hear that Jennifer was dead or at least dying, judging from the way Clara was carrying on.

"Jennifer's not coming to my party! She can't do that, Mom! Best friends are supposed to be there for you always. They're not supposed to go away when you need them most!"

"Clara, her family has been planning this trip for a long time. It's not Jen's fault that. . . ."

"I don't care! He should be here! It's not fair! How could he do that to me?"

"Clar, really. . . . Wait a minute. What did you just say?"

Clara looked at her mom, puzzled. "I said, 'How could she do that to me?'"

"No, you didn't, Clara. You said 'he'—*he* should be here. How could he do that to me?' I think I'm getting the picture now. This isn't about Jennifer. This is about your dad."

"Dad? I'm ready to die 'cause my best friend is deserting me on the most important day of the year, and you're talking about Dad? I don't get it."

"Clara, you have never once talked about your dad's leaving—to me or to anyone. Pretending that you don't feel anything will not make the hurt and anger go away. Look, why don't you go to your room and use some of your things to find a way to let your feelings out?"

"Mom, I don't want to. Oh, what's the use?" Clara stomped out of the kitchen and up to her room. She was so angry she didn't know what to do first. She felt like she wanted to kick and scream and throw things. Instead, she hopped onto her bed and started punching her pillow as hard as she could. "I want Jennifer to come to my party," she yelled. "I want . . . I want . . . I want my daddy to come home!" Finally, after all the weeks of holding it inside, Clara began to cry.

After a while, she went to the closet and got out her Feelings Box. Inside were some special things to help her express her feelings. There was a box of tissues, some drawing paper and markers, a notebook and pen and some stationery.

She looked at each item carefully and then opened the stationery box. The paper had brightly colored balloons in the corner, and it was her favorite. She picked up the pen and wrote, "Dear Daddy," on the first line. Then she spent a long time writing everything she was feeling in a long, long letter—four whole pages! When she was all done, she folded the letter, put it in an envelope, and tucked it inside her top dresser drawer, under her socks. She sighed very deeply and said, "I'll decide what to do with it tomorrow." Then she went into the living room and phoned Jennifer.

What do you think?

▸ Why did Clara get so mad when Jennifer couldn't come to her party?
▸ Besides actually sending the letter to her dad, what else might Clara choose to do with it?

▶ If you had a Feelings Box like Clara's, what items would you put in it? What things would help you express your feelings in your way?

Remember...

**You can find your own way to
express your feelings.**

And don't forget that telling your feelings to God is an important part of expressing them. Listen to these words written by King David in the Book of Psalms:

I cry out to the Lord. . . . I pour out my problems to him. I tell him my troubles. When I am afraid, you, Lord, know the way out. **Psalm 142:1–3a** (ICB)

Growing Together

BUILDING ON GOD'S WORD

Write a Family Psalm. Honestly expressing all our feelings to God is an important way for us to handle our feelings. Writing the poems and songs that we can find in the Book of Psalms was David's way of expressing his feelings to the Lord. Involve your family in writing a psalm by copying the following outline onto a large poster board and working together to fill in the blanks. Brainstorm possibilities for each blank and then make a family decision about which words to use. When you are finished, use the Family Psalm for a time of worship and prayer. You can have all family members say it together as a prayer, or follow the directions on the left and use it as a choral reading. Either way, it will be a personal expression to God of your family's feelings and experiences.

ALL: O Lord, You are my _____ and my _____.
You understand all my feelings.

PARENTS: When I feel _____, You _____.

KIDS: When I feel _____, You _____.

ALL: There is nothing I can do that will ever stop You from loving me.

SOLO: Even when I _____, You still love me.

DUET: And when I _____, You still love me.

Growing Together

ALL: Thank You for always being with me!

MALES: When I _____, You are with me.

FEMALES: And when I _____, You are with me.

ALL: O Lord, You are my _____ and my_____.
You understand all my feelings.

CONVERSATION STARTERS

Where Do I Feel It? Our bodies are valuable sources of information about whether we are expressing our feelings or stuffing them inside. You can teach your children to read the signals their bodies give them by drawing one or more simple figures on a piece of paper (older children can make their own drawings) and then talking about the following:

1. What signals do our bodies give us that we have feelings that need to be expressed? As you think of things, draw something on your figure to represent it. For instance, tears around the eyes represent feeling sad, shaky knees represent feeling scared, a knot or butterflies in the stomach represent feeling pressured, and so on.

2. What signals tell us we are stuffing, instead of expressing our feelings? Again, draw something to indicate these symp-

Growing Together

toms. Examples would be headaches, stomachaches, nightmares, feeling chilled, and so on.

3. Ask family members to share ways they would most like to express their feelings (such as physical exercise, writing, talking).

4. Have all members identify one feeling that is hard for them to express. Then ask everyone to set a goal to express that feeling in a new way by completing the following goal statement:

The next time I feel _____, I will express it by
_____

Make an agreement to hold each other accountable for keeping these goals.

FAMILY NIGHT ACTIVITIES

1. Assemble Feelings Boxes. All members of your family can have their own Feelings Box, like the one Clara had in the story. Provide boxes and a variety of items to place inside, such as drawing paper and markers or paints, notebooks, stationery, pens, running shoes, a box of tissues, and so on. Let family members decorate their boxes and then choose and place inside several items they would most like to use to express their feelings. The boxes should be stored in a place where they can be easily accessed when needed.

Growing Together

2. Make a Feelings Volcano. Here is a fun activity to dramatize the effect of stuffing our feelings inside. (A parent should decide which children are old enough to make their own volcano.) For each volcano you will need:

- ▸ Modeling clay
- ▸ Small Styrofoam ball
- ▸ 1/8 cup baking soda
- ▸ 1/4 cup liquid detergent
- ▸ 1/3 cup vinegar

Use the modeling clay to fashion a cone-shaped container (the size of a one-cup measuring cup) to hold the other ingredients. With the point of a pencil, draw a person's body (with the heading missing) on the outside of the clay container. Put the baking soda and liquid detergent inside. Finally, draw a face on the Styrofoam ball and position it on top of the cone, forming a whole body.

Brainstorm situations that illustrate stuffing our feelings inside. Here are two to get you started:

▸ The boy in the next seat looked at your paper during a test at school, but you got sent to the principal's office for cheating—for the fourth time this month. When you got home and Mom said, "How was your day?" you just smiled and said, "Fine. What's for dinner?"

▸ Your best friend just told you she is moving to another state. You say, "Wow, neat! Let's go get an ice cream cone."

When your family has thought of several examples, remind them that stuffing feelings does not get rid of them. They stay inside until they find some way to get out. At this point, lift the Styrofoam head, pour the vinegar into the container and quickly replace the head. What happens next is an illustration of what can happen when we try to keep our feelings stuffed inside too long!

End your time by enjoying a cup of "steaming" hot chocolate or apple cider. (If it is summer and "steamy" enough outside, you might want to make homemade lemonade instead!)

C H A P T E R

T H R E E

Keep Out!

GETTING READY

What You See Isn't Necessarily What You Get

 o you know anyone who uses a feelings defense? Perhaps you know someone who:

- ▶ Cracks jokes constantly, especially in the midst of a conflict
- ▶ Has problems that always seem to be someone else's fault
- ▶ Never gets angry or seems to be bothered by anything
- ▶ Talks a mile a minute and never lets anyone respond

These are examples of people who use what is known as feelings defenses. We call certain behaviors "defensive" because that is exactly what they are—a way to defend or protect us from life's most painful and threatening experiences. Feelings defenses work as decoys or distractions, keeping the focus away from whatever feels threatening or painful. When a person is using defensive behavior, what we see in terms of outward behavior may be very different from what the person is actually feeling inside. For instance, in the examples above, what we see is:

- A comedian, or clown
- A poor soul who is always caught in everyone else's ineptitude
- A likable person with an easygoing personality
- A chatterbox

What is real for these people, however, may be something very different. We may actually be relating to individuals who are struggling with some of life's most difficult and painful experiences—and never know it!

People use many defensive behaviors. Common ones are:

- Clowning
- Lying
- Blaming
- Silence or withdrawal
- Pretending or daydreaming
- Constant talking
- People-pleasing
- "Know it all"-ing
- Aggression

In effect, a feelings defense is any behavior that keeps us from focusing on what is real. Here are the main points to keep in mind about them:

1. **Feelings defenses serve an important purpose.** They can help us cope with the painful or dark side of life by giving us time to gather courage and strength to face whatever life has brought our way. Or we may choose to use our defenses to give us a needed break from the intensity of dealing with

certain situations. But feelings defenses become unhealthy when we use them as a barrier to:

▸ **Keep Out** painful feelings we need to face.
▸ **Keep Out** the real problem so that we never resolve the core issue.
▸ **Keep Out** other people who could help if we would let them.

2. **We all use defensive behaviors to some extent, having formed them when we were very small.** When we were young and life felt threatening or painful, we would sometimes defend ourselves by acting in ways that took the focus off the circumstances causing them—believing that as long as we didn't face them, they weren't really there. Of course, as we learned in the previous chapter, choosing not to face frightening or threatening feelings did not make them go away. They continued to live on inside of us, struggling to get out. In fact, many of us have worked hard all our lives to keep those hurtful feelings covered up and out of sight by becoming more and more skillful in the fine art of using our favorite defenses.

3. **Lowering our feelings defenses is a choice we must make for ourselves.** It is the only way we can allow ourselves to face the frightening feelings and hurtful circumstances behind them and thereby resolve the core issues in our lives.

In our Confident Kids® training seminars, I use a stack of Styrofoam cups to illustrate how this works. The stack represents a person who has many feelings and unresolved issues going on inside (the bottom cups), but is choosing to cover them up with a feelings defense (the top cup). When I hold up the stack of cups, I point out that all we know about this "person" is what we can see on the outside—the feelings defense. What is really going on inside is hidden from the rest of the world, and often from the person as well. We can only find out what is beneath the defense when the person chooses to look carefully at each underlying feeling and reveal it.

At this point in the seminar, I ask the participants to make their own stack of cups, representing how they use feelings defenses. I have been amazed at some of the stories I have heard as we shared this experience. Some of the stacks have been as high as ten cups! One woman held up a stack of just three cups, but she gave us a perfect illustration of how feelings defenses work. This was her story:

▸ **Feelings Defense: Perfectionism/Angel.** "I was a perfect little angel in school," she began. "Every teacher's dream student! I obeyed all the rules, did all my work—perfectly, of course—and never caused any problems. That pattern continued into my adult life. I was the perfect college student and perfect employee and so on—until one day I was in a small group setting when another group member yelled at me for doing something wrong. I almost had a nervous breakdown over it, so I decided it was time to get help."

▸ **Feeling #1: Fear.** Removing the top cup, she revealed her first underlying feeling. "With the help of a trusted friend and counselor," she continued, "I began for the first time in my life to lower my defense and look closely at what was behind my perfectionism. What I found was my mother, who was verbally abusive, and of whom I had been deeply afraid for as long as I can remember. Finally, at age twenty-eight, I understood that my perfectionism came from the deep need to do everything right—not because I was such a terrific kid, but so that no one would ever have a reason to yell at me the way my mother did!"

▶ **Feeling #2: Unworthiness/Shame.** Showing us the last cup in her stack, she said, "Getting through the fear was the hardest thing I've ever done. Now I understand why. All those years of verbal abuse left a deep sense of unworthiness and shame at the very center of my being. No amount of acting as the perfect angel could ever hide the most threatening feeling of all—the internalized belief that what I *really* was, was a no-good, rotten little girl, and I always would be.

"As hard as it was to lower my defenses, what I can say now is that I'm wonderfully free—from both the need to be the perfect little angel and the belief that I was a rotten, no-good person."

Learning about feelings defenses is important for two reasons. First, it helps us see the need to lower our own defenses so we can face what is real and resolve the core issues in our lives. Second, it also helps us see defensive behavior in our children so we can help them recognize and lower their defenses now, while they are still forming them. Then we can help them learn to get their needs met in healthier ways (the subject of the next chapter).

For Reflection

1. What feelings defense do you use most often? Describe your earliest memory of using it.

   _____

   _____

   _____

   _____

   Describe at least three other times during your childhood or adolescence when you used it.

   _____

   _____

   _____

   _____

2. For each memory listed above, identify the feelings and painful or threatening experiences you were defending against.

   _____

   _____

   _____

   _____

3. Describe a time in adulthood when you used a feelings defense. Include the circumstances that triggered your defensive behavior and how it kept you from getting your needs met.

   _____

   _____

   _____

   _____

Now list three things you can do in the future to lower your defenses and deal with what is real.

_____

_____

_____

Building On God's Word

We build our feelings defenses out of fear that certain emotions will destroy us or our relationships if we allow ourselves to feel them. David was well acquainted with such fears and expressed them often in the Book of Psalms. Although familiar to most of us, Psalm 23 takes on a whole new meaning when we apply it to lowering our feelings defenses. Read it now, paying particular attention to this verse:

> Even though I walk through the valley of the shadow of death, I will fear no evil, for you are with me; your rod and your staff, they comfort me. *Psalm 23:4*

You can make David's prayer your own as you walk through the valley of lowering your defenses and facing the painful feelings and frightening circumstances that are behind them.

etting Up Barriers

Have you ever seen a big **Keep Out!** sign anywhere? You might have seen one at a construction site, warning people that it would be dangerous to walk through that place. Or you've seen a sign that says **Private** on an office door, which is a way to say, "Go away. I don't want to be bothered," to everyone who sees it. Or maybe your brother has a big **Keep Out!** sign on his bedroom door—and you know what that means!

We use **Keep Out!** signs as barriers to keep people out of the places where we do not want them to go. When we hang a **Keep Out!** sign on our door, we are telling everyone around us that we just want to be left alone.

Sometimes we may wish that we could use a **Keep Out!** sign to make certain feelings leave us alone. Wouldn't it be nice if, whenever we felt frightened or hurt, we could just put up a big sign that says:

"Keep Out! I don't want to feel you—so just stay away!"

Actually, you probably do have ways of keeping out certain feelings, and you don't even know it. You don't use a real sign, of course, but you may do something to protect or defend yourself from certain feelings—like pretending you are not feeling a certain feeling, or not letting anyone else know what you are feeling. This is called using a "feelings defense," and it works just like using a big **Keep Out!** sign. It is a way of telling our feelings to stay away, and telling others around us to stay away, too.

57 ▶

There are many kinds of "keep out" actions, or feelings defenses. Here are just some of the ones people use:

▶ **Clowning.** Making jokes or doing something funny whenever we feel uncomfortable.

▶ **Pretending or daydreaming.** Making-believe we don't feel hurt, or "tuning-out" by thinking of other things when we don't want to feel something.

▶ **Silence or withdrawal.** Never talking about feelings, even if asked. Spending long hours alone reading or watching TV when we don't want to feel something.

▶ **Blaming.** Avoiding hurtful feelings by making everything someone else's fault.

▶ **People-pleasing.** Doing everything other people want you to do, just so they won't ever get mad at you or do something else to make you feel bad.

▶ **Can you think of others?** _____

Everyone uses such "keep out" actions from time to time—and that's okay. But if we use feelings defenses too often, we may end up

keeping out more than is really healthy for us,
for then we may:

▶ **Keep Out** painful feelings we need to face
and express before they come out in ways we
can't control.
▶ **Keep Out** the real problem so it never gets
solved.
▶ **Keep Out** other people who could help.

In the next chapter, we'll discover how we can
lower our defenses and face our feelings in
healthier ways. But first, let's practice identifying some "keep out" actions. Look at each of
these cartoons and write the name of the
defense that is being used on the line below it.

1. Defense _____ **2.** Defense _____

3. Defense _____

4. Defense _____

Here's a story about a boy who used a feelings defense to keep out his real feelings.

The Clown

It was Saturday, Arlo's favorite day of the week, and he was doing his favorite thing—walking to the playground with his best buddy,

61 ▶

Reggie. It was a perfect day, and as usual, Arlo was blabbing on and on about nothing in particular. What was so great about Reggie was that he would listen to you, no matter what you were saying!

But Arlo was so busy talking and making jokes, he didn't notice that Reggie wasn't really listening. He was just staring at the cracks in the sidewalk until he finally looked up and said, "Arlo, would you just shut up long enough for me to tell you something!"

Something about the look on Reggie's face scared Arlo. *Uh-oh*, he thought, *something's wrong here. I'm afraid of what he's going to tell me. It might be bad news, or worse yet, something he's mad at me about! I don't want to hear anything bad, so I'm just going to keep everything funny.* Just as he thought that, something strange happened. His nose started to glow a little bit as he said, "Reg, I just want to tell you one more thing. Okay? Did you hear that Mike Becker brought his frog to school yesterday and it got loose in the cafeteria? Mrs. Brooks. . . ."

"Just shut up, Arlo! Everyone knows about

that stupid frog! I'm trying to tell you something important."

"Okay, I get the message! What's more important than Mike Becker's frog?"

Reggie took a deep breath and then blurted out, "My dad told us at breakfast this morning that we have to move to Texas. He's got a different job and he starts next month. We'll be moving in three weeks!"

Oh, I knew it was something bad, I just knew it! Arlo groaned inside himself. Reggie is my best friend in the whole world, and I don't think I can live without him! How could this happen? This hurts too much for me to face. I won't let myself think about this. As he thought these things, his nose changed even more. Now it was bright red and shaped just like a clown's nose: fat and round.

"Hey, Reg, that's neat!" Arlo said with a big smile on his face. "Are you gonna have your own horse and everything? I can see you now, walking bowlegged and wearing a ten-gallon cowboy hat."

Reggie stared at his friend. "How can you be so cheerful? I thought you were my best friend!

Don't you understand? We aren't going to be together anymore!"

Now a big clown smile started to form on Arlo's mouth. "I heard," he said. "But Mike Becker's frog was more exciting. Did you hear it even got in the soup? Everyone was screaming and. . . ."

Reggie looked away from Arlo and started to cry. "I thought you were my friend," he said, "but I guess I was wrong. You don't even care that I'm moving away or that we won't be together or that I feel hurt. All you ever do is make dumb jokes and laugh! I hate you, and I'm glad I'm moving away!" Then he turned around and started running home.

Arlo stared after him for a long time. Slowly the clown face started to fade as he thought, *I really blew it this time. Now my best friend is not only moving away, but he hates me, too. I feel like I want to die! I don't know what to do with all this hurt I'm feeling. Maybe I should run after Reg and tell him how I feel.* Arlo was so deep in thought that he never heard Mike Becker come up behind him.

"Hey, Arlo, what's happening?" Mike asked.

"You look real sad. Is something wrong?"

Arlo stared blankly at Mike for just a moment. Then he smiled and said, "Aw, it's nothing much. Not compared to what happened in the cafeteria yesterday! That's the most fun I've had in a long time. Did you ever get your frog back? Or did it drown in the soup?" The boys linked arms and started out for the swing set, Arlo's face once again looking like the neatest clown face you ever saw.

What do you think?

▶ Why did Arlo start using the feelings defense of being a clown?

▶ How did using this defense hurt his relationship with his best friend? How did it keep him from getting his own needs met?

▶ Tell about a time you used a feelings defense to cover up or keep out a scary or hurtful feeling.

Remember . . .

You can choose to lower your defenses and tell others what you need.

You use your defenses when you feel frightened or in pain. Knowing that God is with you and promises to guide and protect you during those times can help. Here's a verse from the Bible to remember:

Even if I walk through a very dark valley, I will not be afraid because you are with me. *Psalm 23:4a* (ICB)

Growing Together

BUILDING ON GOD'S WORD

Psalm 23:4 Mural. You will need a three-to four-foot length of butcher or shelf paper, water-base markers (permanent ones will bleed through onto the wall or floor), cotton balls, and glue.

Read Psalm 23:4 to your family and talk about it as follows:

1. In Psalm 23, King David, who was once a shepherd, talks about how God takes care of us just as a shepherd takes care of his sheep. In this verse, he was remembering the times he had to take his sheep through the dark and often dangerous valleys between the mountains. *[Draw a valley on the paper, with a flock of sheep walking through it. Remember, simple lines for mountains and circles with legs for sheep work just fine!]* Why was the valley so dangerous? *[If there are no suggestions, point out that there could be rock slides or wild animals attacking, but nowhere for the sheep to go to get away.]*

2. In our daily lives, we sometimes go through things that feel as scary and dangerous as walking through a dark valley. What has happened to us or might happen in the future that is scary and dangerous? *[As family members think of things, write them on the mountain walls. Examples might be divorce, drugs, alcohol, accidents, moving, gangs, etc.]*

3. But David reminds us that we don't have to be afraid of the scary things in our lives. Why? Because God will be with us. *[Draw a shepherd in the midst of the flock.]* God promises to be with us no matter what happens. He might not always stop bad

Growing Together

things from happening, but nothing will ever stop Him from loving or caring for us. Let's thank Him for that!

End with a prayer of thanks for God's presence and protection in the scary points of our lives. Then let the kids finish the mural by adding some details, coloring it, and gluing cotton balls on the sheep.

CONVERSATION STARTERS

Defense Masks. Prepare a set of masks ahead of time by drawing the following faces on paper plates (the thin ones that bend easily):

Clowning   Denial/Pretending   Blaming   Silence/Withdrawal

Growing Together

Add any others that represent feelings defenses used by your family members. Attach string or yarn so that each plate can be worn as a mask.

Sit your family in a circle around a table or on the living room floor, with the masks in the middle. Now ask for three volunteers to act out the story, "The Clown" (see above). Give "Arlo" the clown mask and have him hold it in front of his face whenever Arlo is using that defense in the story.

After the story, ask your family to think of other defenses Arlo might have used besides clowning, and what he would have said or done for each. For instance, what would Arlo have said to Reggie if his defense was blaming? What might he have done to handle his feelings if his defense was silence, or withdrawal? When you have identified a few defenses and possible behaviors, role-play the story again, using the masks to show Arlo using a number of different defenses.

FAMILY NIGHT ACTIVITIES

Host a Family Game Night. Children love to play games with adults. If your family is small, invite one or two other families to join you to play the following games at your home or in a nearby park.

Growing Together

1. *Hide and Seek.* This classic children's game begins with one person who is "it" counting to one hundred while everyone else scatters to find a hiding place. Then "it" goes seeking the other players, until all are found or a designated time limit is reached. If there are still players who have not been found when the time is up, all the players who have been found cry out, "Olly-olly-oxen-free!" and the remaining players come out from hiding to start a new round.

2. *Sardines.* This is a variation of Hide and Seek, only this time the person who is "it" finds a hiding place and all the other players go looking for him or her. As "it" is found, the players join him or her in the hiding place, squeezing together like sardines. Be prepared for lots of giggles as the hiding place gets fuller and fuller. When all have found the place, start a new round.

3. *Red Rover.* This game works best with a fairly large group (at least eight). Divide into two teams, being sure each team is balanced in terms of size and strength of players. Each team stands in a line facing the other team, at least twenty feet away. To play, one team targets a player from the other line. Then they all hold hands tightly and chant together, "Red Rover, Red Rover, let _____ [the player's name] come over!" The player whose name was called must then run as fast as he can and try to break through the line of the other team. If he is successful, he gets to take someone from that team back to his own line. If he is unable to break through, he must stay and join the team that called him over. Continue play until one team no longer exists.

Growing Together

When you are through playing games, gather everyone together for a simple supper or dessert. As you are eating, have a short discussion, using the following questions.

▶ How did it feel to play *Hide* and *Seek* and not be found? What do you think it would be like to always be hiding and never be found?

▶ How did it feel to play *Sardines* and join in with a whole group of people in the hiding place?

▶ Which was more fun in *Red Rover*—breaking through the line or being held out?

Then point out that these games are a lot like feelings defenses. Keeping our defenses up can be very lonely—like always hiding so well that no one ever finds us. Lowering them is like playing *Sardines*. It feels good to have others close by. *Red Rover* shows how much strength we can have when we all hold on to each other and don't let go, no matter what comes along!

I'm All Shook Up!

GETTING READY

But I Don't Know What I'm Feeling!

Five-year-old Timmy had been warned about throwing things in the house one too many times. So, this time, when he threw something that came dangerously close to breaking a lamp, his mom lost her cool. A loud scolding of "How many times do I have to tell you?" and "You never listen to me!" ended with Tim being sent to his room until further notice. As he stomped loudly away, mumbling such things as "It's not fair!" and "It just slipped out of my hand," he suddenly turned, put his hands on his head, and said, "Oww! My brain feels funny—it gets all scrambled up when you yell at me!"

I can identify with this little guy completely. I've never used the same phrase, but I know exactly what he was talking about. In fact, it's an experience we all share, although we may have different names for it. "My stomach is all in knots," or "I'm losing it," or "I'm all shook up!" are all ways of saying the same thing— we are having an emotional reaction that short-circuits our ability to be clear about what we are feeling or thinking at a given moment. Those times usually feel scary or frightening and are not always easy to get through. When they do come, it is important for us to be able to think clearly enough to realize that we have a choice to make. We can choose to remain in our state of feeling "all shook up" and use a feelings defense to deal with it, or we can choose to listen to our feelings and sort through them to discover what is really going on. But how do we do that?

In this chapter, we will trace the experiences of three people as they work through a four-step process to sort out their feelings. The journey begins for each one as they find themselves looking in the mirror one morning, feeling down, and telling themselves the following messages:

> ▶ **Sheila:** "I'm fat and ugly and that's the way I'm *always* going to be!"
> ▶ **Thomas:** "I'm *never* going to amount to anything. Nothing I ever do is right."
> ▶ **Jana:** "Poor Jason will *never* amount to anything as long as he has me for a parent!"

Telling themselves these kinds of "global" (notice the words *always* and *never*) and "self-destructive" messages was a signal to all three of these people that they had scrambled feelings inside that need to be sorted out. Rather than believing these first messages or feeling overwhelmed by them, they took the time to sort them out by using four simple steps.

Step One: Identify the source of the feeling(s). When we feel a barrage of "scrambled" feelings, it can seem so overwhelming that we may not know where to begin to sort them out. Questions such as *"When* did I start feeling this way?" and *"What happened* that started this feeling?" can give us the information we need. Identifying a particular time and event keeps us focused on what is real and avoids wasting time and energy on global and self-destructive messages. Notice how each of our three people changed their initial messages to clear statements focused on specific times and events:

> **Sheila:** "I've felt awful ever since I ate that hot fudge sundae at lunch yesterday."
> **Thomas:** "I started losing it as soon as my parents arrived for dinner last night."
> **Jana:** "It all started when the principal from Jason's school called on Monday."

Step Two: Accurately name the feeling(s) involved. There is tremendous power in naming what is real. As we learned in the first chapter, feelings are valuable sources of information and energy, but only when we know what they are. And, as we saw in the second chapter, feelings must be appropriately expressed before they will "go away."

Naming feelings accurately takes some practice. Saying that we feel "awful" or are "losing it" is too vague to be helpful. Our task is to pinpoint the precise feelings that have been aroused by the circumstances and events identified in step one. Using a list of "feelings" words such as the one on pages 22-23 can help. As we read through the list, certain words will seem to "pop off the page." We can keep working at it until there is an assurance deep inside that says, "Yes! That is exactly what I am feeling!" In our three examples, the feelings that each person named were:

> **Sheila:** Guilt, shamed, and dominated.
> **Thomas:** Stupid, bad, and threatened.
> **Jana:** Failure, confused, and shamed.

Step Three: Decide what to do about the feeling(s). Once we know exactly what feelings we are dealing with, we must make some choices. Examples of choices you might make to deal with your feelings are:

- Find a healthy way to express it (see chapter 2).
- Make amends when you have been wrong.
- Choose to reject inappropriate and self-destructive messages.
- Find a trusted friend or counselor or support group to help you understand the source of your feelings.
- Make an action plan. For example, call a friend if you feel lonely.

Here are the choices the people in our examples made to deal with their feelings:

Sheila was surprised that feeling "dominated" surfaced in step two. Thinking about that helped her see that she had ordered the hot fudge sundae at lunch as a reaction to the fight she had had with her husband the night before, in which she had felt completely dominated by him. For the first time in her life, she began to wonder if she was using food as an inappropriate way to deal with her feelings—a cycle that increased her feelings of shame and guilt, since she had struggled with being overweight all her life. She decided to find a counselor to help her work through these issues.

Thomas had already been working on recognizing the self-destructive messages that were often triggered by his encounters with his overdemanding parents. He first of all chose to reject the negative messages, and then made an action plan that included time to journal his feelings and specific ways to celebrate the relationships in his life that reminded him of how worthwhile and valuable he really is.

Jana decided to take a risk by making an appointment to see the principal and telling him how confused she was about being a parent. (Jason had been born when Jana was only seventeen.)

Although sharing her true feelings was not easy for her, she was able to give him a clear statement of her feelings of shame that Jason was constantly in trouble at school. The principal reminded her that becoming a teenage parent presented special problems and referred her to a parents' group that met at a nearby community center. From the first meeting, Jana discovered that sharing with others who were struggling with the same issues greatly reduced her feelings of confusion and failure.

Step Four: Follow through with the choice made in step three. There is, of course, a big difference between knowing what to do and doing it. Taking action is a big part of getting through our difficult feelings. As with Jana, it may involve taking risks that feel frightening or difficult. Just remember—if your plan of action feels too threatening, it's always okay to ask for help!

Learning the skills of sorting out our feelings may take some practice and patience at first, but it is well worth the effort. As parents, there is a double reason to do so. Not only is it healthy for us, but we will only be able to help our children work through their feelings when we have first learned the skills of working through our own.

For Reflection

1. Describe a time in your childhood or adolescence when you felt you had "a scrambled brain" or "knots in your stomach," or you were "losing it," and you didn't know why.

_____

_____

_____

2. Describe a recent time when you had the same experience.

_____

_____

_____

_____

Do you see any connection between the two experiences?

_____

_____

_____

_____

3. Now use the four steps to work through the experiences you described in (1) and (2):

Step One: Identify the source of the feeling(s).

(1) _____

(2) _____

Step Two: Accurately name the feelings involved.

(1) _____

(2) _____

Step Three: Decide what you can do (or could have done) about the feeling(s).

(1) _____

(2) _____

Step Four: If it is still possible, do it!

Building On
God's Word

Honestly facing your feelings is a powerful form of truth-telling. Read the Bible verses below, applying them to the experience of letting go of your feelings defenses and telling the truth about what is behind them.

> Surely you desire truth in the inner parts; you teach me wisdom in the inmost place. Psalm 51:6

> Jesus said, "If you hold to my teaching, you are really my disciples. Then you will know the truth, and the truth will set you free." John 8:31–32

If you are struggling with telling yourself the truth "in the inner parts," notice that God promises to guide you through your journey. Bring your struggles to Him in prayer now, asking for His wisdom to lead you to the truth that will set you free.

Detecting the Evidence

Do you like mystery stories? Or have you ever played the game *Clue?* It can be fun to look for clues and try to figure out what really happened in a story. Sometimes the clues are obvious and it's easy to solve the mystery. Other times there may not be very many clues and it seems as though we'll never be able to figure things out or find the culprit.

Handling our feelings can sometimes be like

solving a mystery. In fact, learning to be a "feelings detective" is a healthy skill to learn! It's a skill we need whenever someone asks us, "What are you feeling?" and all we can think of to say is, "Yucky," or "In the pits," or "Who cares!". We all have lots of times when we feel yucky or in the pits and don't really know why. When we feel awful and don't know why, it's usually because we have so many feelings going on inside that they get all scrambled up. That can feel so scary or powerful, we want to use a feelings defense to pretend everything is okay. But, as we learned in the previous chapter, using "keep out" behavior can often hurt us more than help us. It's much better to become feelings detectives and take the time to solve the case of "What Am I Feeling?" than to bury the evidence. There are four steps we can follow to learn to be good feelings detectives. It works like this:

Step One: Use detective questions to find clues. Ask yourself:

▶ **When** did I start feeling this way?

▶ **Where** was I?

_____

▶ **Who** else was involved?

_____

▶ **What** happened?

_____

▶ **Why** did this upset me so much?

_____

_____

_____

_____

What clues can you find that can help Abigail
sort out what she is feeling?

▶ **When** she started feeling awful

_____

▶ **Who** else was involved

_____

▶ **What** happened

_____

▶ **Why** it upset her

_____

Step Two: Name the exact feelings.
Remember what we learned in the first chapter
about how all our feelings can help us—but only
when we know what they are? And in the next
chapter we learned that feelings stay inside
until we find the right way to express them. The
only way we can do either of those things is to
name exactly what we are feeling. That can take
some time and practice, but after a while,
naming our feelings gets easier.

What feelings do you think Abigail is
having about the fight her parents had?

_____

Step Three: Decide what to do about the feelings. Once we know what we are feeling, we can make a choice about what to do. Here we must be careful, because sometimes the first thing we may want to do is to use a defense so we don't have to face our feelings. It's important to think about all the ways we could handle the feelings we named—and choose one that is healthy.

Which of Abigail's choices is the healthiest?

_____

Step Four: Do it! Deciding what to do and doing it are not always the same thing. Following through can be hard.

As hard as it may be, taking action about our feelings is always better than keeping them locked up inside. Remember, you can always ask for help if you need it.

Here's a story about a boy who learned to use the four steps to becoming a feelings detective:

Following the Footprints of Frenzied Feelers

"Hi! My name is Father Floyd Fowling and I'm famous for finding frenzied feelers and helping them become healthy, forthright feelers. In fact, I've been fast following a frenzied feeler for five hours. Ah, I say there, fellow, would you favor me with a few moments of your time?"

"You talkin' to me?"

"Yes, my fine friend. You look frightfully frazzled, and I'd like to remove the frown from your face."

"But I don't even know you."

"A fine point! My name is Father Floyd Fowling, and I am famous for finding frenzied feelers and helping them become healthy, forthright feelers. And you look about as frantic a feeler as I've ever found."

"Glad to know you, I think. My name is Fred, and I haven't the faintest idea what a 'frenzied feeler' is, so how do I know if I'm one or not?"

"A fundamental figure of speech to fix firmly in our minds before formulating our plan. A 'frenzied feeler' is someone who is feeling something—probably lots of somethings—but can't figure out what the feelings are all about."

"Ah. So, if I can tell you what I'm feeling, then I'm not a frenzied feeler?"

"Fast learner, aren't you?"

"Well, frankly, I'm feeling yucky. Maybe the yuckiest I've ever felt in my whole life."

"That's about as frenzied a response as I've ever found anywhere. So, may we forge forward with my famous four steps for turning frenzied feelers into forthright feelers?"

"Sure, I guess so. Can't hurt, 'cause I feel so feeble now that even *you* couldn't make me feel worse."

"Fascinating! Now, step one is to *use detective questions to find clues*. So, Fred, what happened today that started this feeling? Fire away with all the facts—like who, what, where, when, why."

"Nothin' happened that I can think of. I just did the usual dumb stuff. School was sort of boring, but. . . ."

"You failed to follow up with some facts, Fred. Did something fortuitous happen at school today?"

"Naw. Unless maybe you count the not-so-fine grade I got on my spelling test."

"A fact not to be forgotten! Like, how 'not-so-fine'?"

"Like, I missed fourteen words."

"How fierce! And how many words were on the test?"

"Like, fourteen."

"Uh-huh! Now we're finding fabulous facts for solving this case. So, let's forge forward with step two, which is to *name the exact feeling.* Can you tell me exactly what you are feeling? Besides 'yucky,' that is."

"Well, let's see. 'Yucky' isn't good enough, huh? How 'bout forlorn, fractured, and fuzzy? Any of those getting close?"

"Fiendishly sorry, but I must ask you to be more frank and precise."

"Okay, okay, let's see. I'm sad. Yeah, that's it! Uh, well, maybe that's not it exactly. I feel depressed. No, that's not quite it either. I guess I feel mostly *foolish.* Bingo, Father Flower! That's exactly what I'm feeling—foolish!"

"The name's Fowling, Fred. So, you feel foolish. That's fine!"

"Hey. . . ."

"No, no, I don't mean "fine" that you're foolish—I mean feeling foolish. I mean 'fine' that you know you're foolish—no, I mean it's fantastic that you *feel* foolish. What I mean to say is. . . ."

"Look, Father Flaking, if you're supposed to be cheering me up, all I can say is, you've just flipped me a foul ball."

"Fowling, the name's Floyd Fowling! Oh, forget it. Let's just forge forward. So, you're feeling ferociously foolish because you flunked your spelling test today. Were the fourteen words too hard for you?"

"Yup! Well, that's not quite fair. To be frank, I guess I just didn't study them fully."

"A forthright answer! I feel you're ready to face step three, which is to *decide what to do about the feeling*. What do you think, Fred?"

"I kind of want to go to my room and cry."

"A fitting possibility. Any other feasible ideas?"

"I could bring my teacher a bag of frosted fudge brownies. She loves frosted fudge brownies!"

"My, my—bribery! Feel free to keep thinking."

"I suppose you want me to say I could go home and study my spelling words."

"A fabulous idea! Now, are you finally ready for step four?"

"Which is?"

"DO IT!"

"Okay, okay, you don't have to yell! Let's see, I think 'frightfully' is one of my words this week. F-r-y-t-f-u-l-l-e-e. I think that's right, but I'll check it as soon as I find my spelling book! 'Bye, Father Flubber—and thanks!"

"Ah, the name is . . . no matter! Because once again I, Father Floyd Fowling, have faced a forlorn fellow and used my famous four steps to turn this frenzied feeler into a healthy, forthright feeler! Now, if I could only find a formula to fix his spelling! Good fortune to you, Fred!"

What do you think?

▶ What was Fred's problem?

▶ Review the four steps Father Fowling used to help Fred handle his feelings in a healthy way.

▶ Describe a time recently when you have been a frenzied feeler like Fred. Try using

Father Fowling's famous four steps to help you handle your feelings right now!

Remember ...

You can face your feelings openly— instead of covering them with a defense.

Facing your feelings is a way of telling the truth to yourself and others. Sometimes, though, it is hard to know exactly what you are feeling on the inside. At those times, you can ask God to help you know. Here's a promise from the Bible to remember:

> Surely you desire truth in the inner parts; you teach me wisdom in the inmost place. *Psalm 51:6*

Growing Together

BUILDING ON GOD'S WORD

Memorize Key Verses. Learning special Bible verses gives family members the truths of God's Word in a form that will always be available to them. Around the dinner table, in the car, or at bedtime are good times to learn and review the key verses from this book: Joshua 1:9; Psalm 142:1–3a; 23:4; and Psalm 51:6. This can be turned into a fun family project by using Bible memory games. Here are two games you might try:

Family Circle. One person in the family starts off by saying the first word of a Bible verse. The next person must say the second word, and so on around the circle. If someone misses, the next person must start over with the first word. Continue until the whole verse, including the reference, can be said around the circle quickly and easily.

Verse Race. Make two or more identical sets of memory cards by cutting 3" x 5" cards in half and printing one word of a Bible verse on each card in a set, including the reference. Mix the cards up and give a set to each person (or team of two) and then race to see who can put the verse in order the quickest.

Growing Together

CONVERSATION STARTERS

Watch TV Together. Choose a favorite family TV show and make a date to watch it together. As you watch, have everyone work together to make a list of the following:

1. The different feelings you observe being experienced by the characters
2. Example(s) of a character who is using a feelings defense
3. Example(s) of a character who is handling a feeling in a healthy way
4. Example(s) of a character handling a feeling in an unhealthy way

When the show is over, talk about your list. Give particular attention to numbers 2 and 4, asking family members to suggest healthier ways the characters could have handled their feelings.

FAMILY NIGHT ACTIVITIES

1. Create Silly Stories. Children enjoy the variety and humor of this activity. Begin with five lunch-size paper bags, numbering them 1 through 5. Then copy the following names or phrases on separate slips of paper, fold them up, and place them in the appropriate bag.

Growing Together

Bag #1: Names

Names of your child(ren)'s teacher(s), coach(es), etc.

Names of all family members

Names of various neighbors and family friends

Names of family pet(s)

Name of your pastor

Name of your boss (and your spouse's boss)

Names of familiar fictional heroes and cartoon characters

Bag #2: Feelings

Angry

Sad

Embarrassed

Proud

Joyful

Jealous

Lonely

Loved

Scared

Guilty

Worried

Stupid

Disappointed

Grateful

Hurt

(Add any other "feelings" words your family will particularly relate to.)

Growing Together

Bag #3: Verbs

Climbed
Fought
Bought
Rode
Lost
Yelled at
Jumped over
Sat on
Read
Sold
Ate
Found
Kissed
Wrote on
Ran up
Cooked
Buried
Swallowed
Tore up
Punched
Hugged
Broke
Planted
Squeezed
Dragged
Fixed
Tossed
Ruined

Bag #4: Nouns
Tree
Nail
Horse
Library book
Chocolate pie
White House
Treasure
Clown
Sailboat
Me
Airplane
$100
Caterpillar
Giraffe
Teacher
Space ship
My bed
Tulip
The President
New York City
Brussels sprout
Roller blades
Bicycle
Cat
Dog
Apple
Spoon
Pillow

Growing Together

Bag #5: Ways to Handle Feelings

Crying

Writing a letter

Running around the block

Taking a bath

Sneezing

Calling a friend

Hiding

Singing

Shouting from the rooftop

Sleeping

Telling a joke

Eating an ice cream cone

Running away

Drawing a picture

Asking for a hug

Breaking a window

Punching his/her pillow

Yelling at a brother or sister

(Add other common ways your family has of handling their feelings)

Now set the bags in the middle of your table or family circle. Let family members take turns drawing one slip from each bag. Use whatever slips were drawn to fill in this short story:

#1 feels   #2 because he/she   #3 [a/the]
#4 . He/she will try   #5 to handle that feeling.

Set the first set of slips aside and draw new ones to make another story. Continue as long as interest holds. Then use one or two of your favorites to talk about how these silly stories all make the same point. It is healthy to handle our feelings by naming a feeling accurately, understanding what caused the feeling, and deciding the best thing to do about the feeling.

2. Make Story Books. An additional way you can use the numbered slips of paper is to lay them all out on the table and let family members take turns choosing one from each category and then add some details to make up their own story about handling feelings. Older children may enjoy writing, illustrating, and binding their stories into books.

CHAPTER

FIVE

The Family That That *Feels* Together, Grows Together

GETTING READY

It All
Sounds Great But—

Our Confident Kids parents' group had been in session about fifteen minutes when one of the parents who had been in the group a long time stumbled in, looking particularly stressed and preoccupied. She didn't speak until near the end of the group time. Then she said, "I had the most awful time getting here tonight. My oldest son, George, was in rare form even for him, and it was a chore just to get him in the car. Then we swung through McDonald's so we could eat supper on the way. As we drove away, it started. George just couldn't keep from harassing his younger brother, Harry, and it was wearing me down. No matter what I said, or how many threats I used, George just kept on and on. The last straw came when I heard Harry say, 'Stop it! That's gross! Just leave me alone!' I looked in the rear view mirror and was horrified to see George stuffing french fries up his brother's nose. I have to admit, I lost it at that point—and it is only by the grace of God that we got here at all!"

She had the whole group with her as she painted this incredible scene, with which every parent in the room could identify to one degree or another. Then she added, "You know, I am so grateful for all the things I've learned in this group. But I have to admit that sometimes when I get to the point of applying it in my own family—well, I just don't know. . . ." and heads nodded all around the room!

Learning to handle feelings is like that. It is difficult enough to manage our own feelings in healthy ways. It is often even harder to deal appropriately with all the feelings in a family setting. At that level, it is very easy to say, "It all sounds great, but putting it into practice in my family—well, that's something else again!" As I have listened to parents struggle with this issue over the years, there have emerged a number of themes that seem to hold the key to successfully managing the feelings experienced in family life. Stated as guidelines, they are as follows:

Guideline #1: **All family members have a right to feel their feelings.** Once we have learned that "all my feelings are okay," the next step is to add, "All your feelings are okay, too." However, believing this and communicating it to others are two different things. If we grew up with lots of messages that denied us our feelings, we may unknowingly be hooked into a communication style that tells others to block or bury their feelings. Notice the difference between the following paired statements:

Responses That Deny Feelings
"Stop that crying! We'll buy another goldfish."

"Scared? There's nothing here to be scared about. Only wimps are afraid of the dark."

"There, there! I'm here, so you don't have to feel sad anymore. I'll take care of you now."

Responses That Validate Feelings
"It hurts a lot to lose a pet, doesn't it?"

"Being alone in the dark does feel scary sometimes. Would having a night light by your bed help?"

"I wish I could take the sadness away, but I can't. It's okay to feel sad right now. Would you like to talk about it?"

Another effective way to validate other people's feelings is just to say, "Uh-huh," or "Really?" while continuing to pay attention to what they are saying. That response not only says it's okay to feel what they are feeling, but it invites them to say more about it. We are affirmed and strengthened by expressing our feelings to another person who is listening attentively and accepting that what we are feeling is real.

Guideline #2: **Feelings must be expressed within certain boundaries.** As we discovered in chapter 2, there is a difference between expressing our feelings in healthy ways and engaging in a feelings free-for-all that is self-destructive, harms someone else, or damages property. To successfully manage feelings in a family setting, it is imperative that all members acknowledge the "rules" about when and where and how they may express their feelings. For example:

▸ When you are angry, you may go to your room and pound your pillow or go to the garage and use the punching bag. But you may not break anything in your room or punch anyone else.

▸ When you feel sad, you may cry, ask to be held, or go to your room to be alone for a while. But you may not call anyone names or pretend to be sick or hide somewhere without telling anyone where you are.

▸ When you feel hurt, you may cry or go to your room and use your Feelings Box to express your pain. You may not ignore us when we ask you what's wrong; instead, you must

use at least one "feeling" word to tell us what's going on.
▶ When there is a disagreement between family members, they will work it out *without* calling each other names, hitting each other, or breaking anything.

Notice that none of the above boundaries denies anyone his or her feelings. They are simply management tools that can help family members express their feelings in healthy, rather than destructive, ways—but only when two principles are *uncompromisingly* followed:

▶ Boundaries must be clearly stated and understood by all family members.
▶ Parents are responsible for seeing that the boundaries are consistently upheld.

Feelings free-for-alls happen when children do not know precisely what is expected of them, or when the rules are enforced sometimes but not at others. Believe it or not, your kids will feel safer and more secure when the adults in their lives hold them accountable for respecting clearly established boundaries.

Guideline #3: **All family members can own what they are feeling.** Owning a feeling means we are "in charge" of that feeling and will assume responsibility for managing it, even though we may need some outside help. Much of the conflict we get into over feelings comes from the way we communicate them to each other. For example, when we are experiencing strong negative emotions, it is easy to use generalizations and statements that blame and/or shame someone else:

- "*You* dumbhead! Why are *you* always touching my stuff? I can't find my skateboard and it's all *your* fault!"
- "Why do *you* guys always bombard me with what *you* want as soon as I walk in the door? Did any of *you* ever once think about anyone but *yourselves?* I'm not going to do another thing for *you* until *you* stop being so selfish!"

In those statements, using accusatory "you" words merely shifts the responsibility for a feeling to another family member, without either identifying the feeling or communicating that the speaker is really asking for help or understanding. Notice the difference in tone when "I" statements are used to express a feeling and clearly say what the speaker needs or wants:

- "*I* feel really upset that *I* can't find my skateboard. Mom says you used it yesterday, and *I'd* appreciate your help in finding it."
- "Work was really stressful today, and *I'm* beat. *I* need a half hour to myself before answering those questions. If you could find something to do, *I'll* be glad to talk later."

These statements are much more effective, since the speaker first claims ownership of a feeling and then makes a straightforward, blame-free request of another person. Owning our feelings is a powerful reminder that although we may be affected by other people's actions, we can maintain control of our own feelings, take responsibility for how we express them, and thereby get help in meeting our needs.

Guideline #4: **Understand emotional temperature and timing.** When tempers are hot is probably not the best time to give lectures or try to talk things out. When hurt and grief are new is definitely not an appropriate time to talk about replacing what was lost or telling jokes to lighten the mood. Sometimes the best thing to do is allow time for emotional temperatures to cool and hurts to begin to heal. Where we often make the biggest mistake, however, is believing that once the precipitating event has passed, it is too late to talk through what happened. Understanding emotional temperature and timing tells us that just the opposite is true. It is very important to come back to the subject at a time when it can be discussed openly and honestly. In fact, it is never too late—in minutes, hours, days, even years—to talk about past conflicts or hurts. It is the only way to achieve complete resolution and then move on.

Managing feelings in a family setting in an open and fair manner is a vital part of having a healthy family. Although this takes lots of time and energy to accomplish, be assured that the end result is well worth the work.

F o r   R e f l e c t i o n

1. Place an X on the line below to indicate how feelings were generally managed in your family as you were growing up.

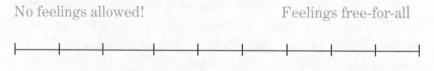

No feelings allowed!   Feelings free-for-all

Feelings allowed within healthy boundaries

Now, using a different color pen or pencil, make another X on the line to indicate how feelings are managed within your present family.

2. Make an X next to the kind of statements that were more common in your family when you were growing up.

_____*Denial* of feelings:
For example, "Stop that crying! There is nothing to cry about"; "Only sissies are afraid of the dark"; "There, there, let me make it all better for you."

_____*Validation* of feelings:
For example, "I know it hurts a lot to lose a pet"; "You must be very disappointed. Do you want to talk about it?"; "I can't take the hurt away, but I'm here if you need me."

Which statements are more common in your family now?
_____Denial   _____Validation

3. Listed below are the four guidelines for managing feelings in your family. Rank each of them for your present family, using the scale below.

1 = We need lots of work in this area!
2 = We need more practice, but we understand the basics.
**3 = Although we aren't perfect, we are doing <u>okay in this</u>
      area.**

_____Guideline #1: All family members have a right to feel their feelings.

_____Guideline #2: Feelings must be expressed within certain boundaries.

_____Guideline #3: All family members can own what they are feeling.

_____Guideline #4: Understand emotional temperature and timing.

4. Knowing that skill development takes time and practice, choose the *one* guideline that seems most important for your family to learn. Then make a commitment to start working on it in a specific way.

Your choice
What is the first step you will take?

Building On God's Word

The words in Ephesians 4:26, 29–32 were written by the apostle Paul as instructions for managing feelings within the church, the family of God. Look at those verses now, applying them to the management of feelings within your own family.

26"In your anger, do not sin": Do not let the sun go down while you are still angry. . . . 29Do not let any unwholesome talk come out of your mouths, but only what is helpful for building others up according to

their needs, that it may benefit those who listen.
^{30}And do not grieve the Holy Spirit of God, with
whom you were sealed for the day of redemption.
^{31}Get rid of all bitterness, rage and anger, brawling
and slander, along with every form of malice. ^{32}Be
kind and compassionate to one another, forgiving
each other, just as in Christ God forgave you
Ephesians 4:26, 29–32

Briefly explain how each of the verses specified below apply to
the guidelines for managing feelings described in this chapter.

▶ Guideline #1—verse 26 _____
▶ Guideline #2—verses 26, 31_____
▶ Guideline #3—verse 29_____
▶ Guideline #4—verse 26_____

It is no accident that verse 32 comes at the end of this passage.
This summarizing principle is clear: **We cannot get to kindness
and compassion and forgiveness until we "get rid" of
feelings such as anger and bitterness.** We know that stuffing
feelings inside and/or covering them with defensive behaviors
does *not* get rid of them. God's Word affirms that dealing with
difficult feelings in healthy ways is the key to successfully
managing feelings in our families.

"Do Unto Others..."

Living together in a family setting isn't always easy. Every family has times when it doesn't seem like much fun to be in it. Brothers and sisters get in each other's way, parents have bad days and yell, fights happen, feelings get hurt. You can probably think of other unpleasant things that happen in your own family.

But did you ever notice that the hardest times of getting along as a family come when strong feelings are involved, like feeling angry or hurt or left out? In fact, knowing what to do when you or other family members are feeling powerful emotions like these will make a big difference in how everyone gets along. Here are two rules that can help you handle those times:

1. **You can express your own feelings without blaming or hurting another person.** Sometimes, the first thing we want to do when we are feeling angry or hurt is to lash out and attack someone else. So, we get into fights or call others names or break something that belongs to them. At the time, it seems like we'll feel better if we do those things. Funny thing is, though, if you express your feelings in that way, you almost always end up feeling worse—and because the other person feels bad, too, the whole situation turns into an awful mess!

   There is a better way. When you are feeling a strong feeling, you can stop long enough to think about what you are feeling and what you may need from another person. Then say something like this:

111 ▶

I feel _____ and I need you to
_____.

Here's an example of how it works.

1.

2.

Don't be discouraged if you don't remember to respond to your feelings in this way at first. You can ask Mom or Dad to help you remember until you can learn to do it on your own.

2. **You can think about what others are feeling and treat them with respect.** When you are feeling strong feelings, you aren't usually thinking about anyone but yourself. Although it is important to think carefully about what you are feeling and how to express it, it also helps a lot to remember that other family members feel the same things you do. Handling feelings in a family is much easier when everyone remembers that no one likes to be made fun of, yelled at, called names, hit, or have his or her things broken. Here are some examples of how life can be much more pleasant when family members try to treat each other the same way they want to be treated:

Here's one for you to try. In the second box,
draw a better way for the brothers to respond.

Living together in families will always have difficult times. But it will help if we learn to handle our feelings in ways that are healthy, which means they are not hurtful to others or ourselves. Here's a story about a family that's having trouble handling their feelings in healthy ways.

The Nice Family

Once upon a time there was a family named Nice who lived in a nice house in a nice neighborhood in a nice town. They even had a nice dog that lived in a nice doghouse in their nice backyard. Everyone on the block thought they were the nicest family around—and said so, in a nice way, of course. In fact, they could have been a perfect family, except for one little problem they had.

115 ▶

The problem was that strange changes were happening to everyone in the Nice family. What kind of changes? Well, first of all the daughter, Nancy Nice, started getting smaller. It all started the night she thought she saw a monster in her room in the middle of the night and screamed for her daddy. When Mr. Nice came in and found out what was wrong, he said, "There are no monsters in here. It's silly to feel afraid, so just go to sleep and don't bother me about monsters again." When he left, Nancy thought she saw the monster again, but now she not only felt scared but very alone, too. She curled up in her bed and felt very small.

The next morning at breakfast, Nick Nice, Nancy's brother—who knew about what had happened because older brothers always know about those kinds of things—said, "Agggh! Look out, Nan, there's a monster under the table! He's going to rip your leg off!" The teasing didn't feel funny to Nancy and she started to cry. Mr. Nice said, "Don't be such a sissy, he's just teasing!" Now the daughter felt really awful, and she discovered that she was even smaller than the night before. But that was okay, because she felt safer when she was small.

Nancy's brother, on the other hand, started growing—of all things—red horns and a red tail. Nick first noticed it the day he brought home the note from his teacher saying he had cheated on a test. He hadn't really cheated, but his teacher hadn't believed him. She said, "It would be just like *you* to do such a thing." Nick didn't know what that meant exactly, but it hurt inside. At home, Mrs. Nice, his mom, said, "Go up to your room, I can't believe a son of mine would act this way. What's wrong with you?" And Mr. Nice said, "I'm ashamed of you. There's nothing worse than a cheater. No son of mine will grow up to be a cheater!" And Nick felt bad inside. That's when he first felt the tiny little horns on his head and the tail poking out behind him. After that, he began to notice just how many times Mom or Dad or someone else was yelling at him for doing bad things—whether or not he had done them—like they just expected him to be bad. Until, finally, Nick started believing that he really must be a bad person. And the horns got bigger and the tail got longer.

Mrs. Nice had a different problem. She was

getting puffy. It all started when she noticed all
the changes happening in her family and it
frightened her. Because she didn't know what to
do about a daughter who was getting smaller
and a son who was growing horns and a tail, she
said, "I'm imagining things!" and stuffed the
feelings inside. "I live in a nice family and have

two nice kids—everyone says so," she said as
she loosened her belt because she was starting
to feel overstuffed. Then, one day, when Mrs.
Nice said to Nancy, "Why can't you ever clean
up your room without my having to tell you?

How can you live in a pig pen like this?" she watched her daughter get smaller right in front of her eyes. That was the greatest hurt of all. It was such a big hurt that Mrs. Nice had to work very hard to stuff it inside, but she did. By now she looked like a blowfish and felt very uncomfortable. Although she was afraid she might explode someday, she wasn't ready to let any of those painful feelings out. So she kept them tightly stuffed inside and got puffier still.

Meanwhile, her husband had problems of his own. Mr. Nice's clothes were being changed into a suit of armor. This started when he saw his daughter looking small and alone but didn't know what to do about it. Sometimes he wanted to put his arms around Nancy and hold her so she wouldn't seem so alone, but he was afraid he would spoil her—so he read the paper instead. And his armor got thicker. Other times he wanted to tell his son how proud he was of him—but that might make Nick soft, and the father knew how important it was to be tough to get along in this world. So Mr. Nice kept on scolding Nick for all the things he did wrong. After all, wasn't that his job as a parent? And he also wanted so much to ask his wife why she was getting puffy, but he was afraid that would make her angry. So he didn't. He just kept on scolding and teasing and reading his newspaper and looking the other way. And the suit of armor got bigger and heavier and clanked a lot.

By now it was getting pretty hard for Mr. and Mrs. Nice and their kids to convince themselves they were still a nice family. It's hard to feel nice when the daughter is very small, the son has horns and a tail, the mom looks like a blowfish, and the dad clanks around in a suit of armor. But they didn't know what else to do, so they just kept on feeling small and bad and uncomfortable and holding their feelings inside—and *pretending* that everyone was feeling nice.

What do you think?
▶ What was happening in the Nice family to cause all the changes?
▶ How could the family members have

handled their feelings in healthier ways?
Using the rules you learned in this chapter,
give some specific examples.

▶ Have you ever felt like anyone in this story?
Who? What happened to make you feel that
way?

Remember . . .

> You can think about your feelings—
> and express them in ways that are
> respectful of others in your family.

This is hard work! But it is also living the way
God teaches us to live. Here are some wise
verses from the Bible:

> When you talk, do not say harmful
> things. But say what people need—
> words that will help others become
> stronger. . . . Never shout angrily or say
> things to hurt others. Never do anything
> evil. Be kind and loving to each other.
> *Ephesians 4:29, 31b, 32a* (ICB)

Growing Together

BUILDING ON GOD'S WORD

Celebrate Joy by Praising the LORD. Much of our discussion in this book has been about handling our difficult feelings. But the Bible has much to say about expressing our joyful feelings, too. Use one of the following activities to have a praise celebration with your family.

Activity #1. **Make a joyful noise to the LORD.** You will need a children's "praise" music tape (ask for help at your local Christian bookstore) and a variety of rhythm band instruments. These can be made easily, using inexpensive household items:

Growing Together

> ▶ A **tambourine** can be made by stapling the edges of two inverted paper plates together after filling the space between them with dried beans.

> ▶ A **drum** can be made from a coffee can or oatmeal box with a plastic lid. Use wooden spoons or dowels as drumsticks.

> ▶ **Sand blocks** can be made by covering wood blocks with sandpaper and then rubbing them together.

> ▶ **Toy kazoos** can be purchased inexpensively from any novelty store.

> ▶ **Bells** can be used in many ways. For example, large jingle bells (strung on a ribbon or sewn to a piece of felt) make a pleasant sound.

By using a little imagination, you can design lots of instruments. Once your rhythm band is ready, begin your praise time. First, read Psalms 100 and 150 and explain that God enjoys hearing our praises. Then start the music tape and let family members sing, play, and dance their praises to God. (Remember, the King James Version of Psalm 100 says to make a joyful *noise* to the LORD!)

Activity #2: **Make Praise Posters.** Even if your family is not musical, you can still have a praise celebration. Begin with reading Psalms 100 and 150, explaining as above. Then use paper, paints, markers, and a variety of art media to create posters proclaiming praise to the LORD. Play a children's worship tape in the background as inspiration and invite family members to sing along while they work on the posters.

End your praise celebration with everyone standing in a circle, holding hands, and thanking God for His blessings and for hearing and delighting in your praises.

CONVERSATION STARTERS

Set Boundaries for Expressing Feelings in Your Family. The best way to be sure everyone in your family understands what the boundaries are is to talk about them and then write them down. Start with a piece of poster board and write across the top: "Expressing Feelings in Our Family." Involve the whole family in the process by asking the following questions:

▸ What are some of the ways we express feelings in our family that cause us problems? (Examples: Hitting or throwing things when angry, pouting and refusing to answer when spoken to, calling names, blaming others, retaliating to "get even.")

▸ How can we express our feelings without being hurtful or disrespectful to someone else?

Since this is probably a time when emotional temperatures are low, you can talk about specific actions that are common in your family. Be sure to describe the behavior without criticizing or blaming the persons involved. Then, using all the information you've talked about, formulate three or four boundaries that will both limit destructive behaviors *and* give choices as to how the feelings can be expressed in healthier ways. (Refer to Guideline

#2 in the "Getting Ready" section of this chapter for examples.) Finally, you will need to talk about what will happen whenever the boundaries are disregarded. Ask all family members for ideas. Just be sure that at the end of this time, kids (especially) are clear that you seriously expect them to respect the boundaries and will hold everyone responsible for doing so.

When the poster is complete, display it in a place where all can see it. This will be helpful when a boundary line is crossed. Family members need only refer to the poster to hold each other accountable to the family "rules" about appropriate ways to express and manage feelings. You can also add more boundaries as the need for them arises.

FAMILY NIGHT ACTIVITIES

Design a Family Celebration. Just as it is important to celebrate our joyful feelings with praise to the LORD, it is equally important to affirm those good feelings through family fellowship. Laughing and playing together are important elements in family health and the foundation for being able to manage the difficult times. Create your own family celebration by combining two or more of the following elements:

1. **Have a Family-Fun Supper.** Plan the menu by asking each family member to choose a favorite food. Be sure to include all these dishes in your supper. Don't expect a balanced

Growing Together

meal—it's okay to have pizza, three desserts, and no vegetables! If you prefer, have a night of "restaurant hopping." Let the kids choose where to go for the main part of the meal, and the parent(s) choose where to go for dessert.

2. **Share Family Memories.** Plan a time to get out all the old scrapbooks, home movies/videos, and photo albums. Enjoy a time of "Remember when . . .' Ask each family member to choose one picture or souvenir that represents his or her most special family memory.

3. **Plan a Family Activity or Outing.** Ask everyone to answer the question, "What do you enjoy doing together as a family more than anything else?" or, "I wish our family would _____ together more often." When all the answers are in, choose one and make specific plans to do that thing or go to that place as soon as possible. (Keep a record of all the "wishes" for future reference.

   Celebrate Your Extended Family. If you have other relatives (or very close friends) in the area, invite them to join you for one or all of the above activities.

5. **Enjoy a Family Hug.** Stand in a circle with your arms around each other's shoulders. After Mom and/or Dad express words of appreciation for each other and for the children, everyone squeezes together in a big hug. (The kids might want to "appreciate" their parents and each other, too!)

S U M M A R Y

*L*earning that "all my feelings are okay" can be both an exciting and a difficult experience. Here are the key points to guide you and your family on this journey:

▸ Feelings send out the messages you need to experience life fully and meet all its challenges.

▸ There are many healthy ways to express your feelings, but only you can decide which ones work best for you.

▸ When feelings seem confusing and overwhelming, you can sort them through and face them openly, instead of hiding behind a feelings defense.

▸ Managing family relationships is easier if all members treat the feelings of others with respect and acknowledge their own feelings without blaming, shaming, or otherwise hurting someone else.

And above all else . . .

. . . remember that God understands everything you feel, and promises to give you peace when you express your feelings openly to Him:

Do not worry about anything. But pray and ask God for everything you need. And when you pray, always give thanks. And God's peace will keep your hearts and minds in Christ Jesus. The peace that God gives is so great that we cannot understand it. *Philippians 4:6–7 (ICB)*

For information about starting a Confident Kids® support group in your community, write:

CONFIDENT KIDS®
% The Recovery Partnership
P. O. Box 11095
Whittier, CA 90603

STAGES OF SKILL DEVELOPMENT

The key point to remember as you start using any of the family guides in this series is this:

**Learning new skills takes time
and feels uncomfortable at first!**

Remember when you were first learning to ride a bicycle or play a musical instrument or hit a baseball? It took time to perfect the skills you needed to accomplish those tasks, and much of that time was spent in boring practice sessions. You probably went through periods of discouragement and thought you would never improve. But persistence and practice eventually paid off, especially if the learning process was a group experience that took place in a friendly environment where everyone's efforts were treated with respect. It helped even more if you were guided by someone who had already mastered the skill and encouraged your every sign of progress.

Developing healthy life skills in a family setting is like that. Learning to live together in new ways will take time and commitment and patience on the part of every family member. Both you and your children will sometimes feel awkward and uncomfortable, as if things will never change for the better.

There are no shortcuts to making healthy life skills a reality in your home, but knowing what to expect can keep you going. Skills development normally occurs in five stages, as the following acrostic illustrates:

S = Seeing the Need
K = Keeping On
I = Increasing Confidence
L = Letting Go
L = Living It

S **Stage 1: Seeing the Need.** All change begins here. It is only when we are motivated by the need for change that we will go through the hard work of learning a new skill.

K **Stage 2: Keeping On.** This is the stage of greatest discouragement and the point at which many people give up. As you start practicing a new skill, it is natural to feel awkward, so you may want to revert to behavior patterns that are familiar and comfortable. At this point, you will need lots of encouragement and the determination to keep going.

I **Stage 3: Increasing Confidence.** Over time, you will begin to see changes, and the ability to use the new skill will take root. Learning to recognize and celebrate small steps of growth will build your confidence and keep you going.

L **Stage 4: Letting Go.** As your skill level improves, more and more you will find yourself letting go of past behavior patterns and replacing them with the new and healthier ones.

L **Stage 5: Living It.** In this last stage, the new skill has become so integrated into your life that it becomes almost automatic. When you find yourself using it easily, you realize that the hard work of the earlier stages has paid off!

RULES FOR FAMILY INTERACTION

It must be kept in mind that the family guides are only a tool to help you create times of learning and connectedness in your family. That cannot happen unless the books are used in an atmosphere of openness and safety for all family members. You can make your "growing together" conversations and your Family Night activities times of heart-to-heart sharing and fun for everyone by setting and consistently maintaining the following rules:

▸ **Family Rule #1: Every member will actively participate in all discussions and Family Nights.** This lets everyone know that he or she is an important part of the family. Parents are expected to participate with their children, not sit on the sidelines and watch the action!

▸ **Family Rule #2: All members will show respect for one another's feelings.** Modeling how to identify and talk about feelings is the best way to help your kids open up to you. Although you will need to use some discretion, letting your children know that you, too, feel a wide spectrum of feelings teaches them to acknowledge their own feelings and honor the feelings of others. Mutual respect encourages family members to feel safe enough to share openly. This rule means that no put-downs, name calling, hitting, or other destructive behaviors are allowed during family sharing times!

▸ **Family Rule #3: Everyone will speak only for themselves.** In many families, one member often acts as the spokesperson for everyone else. This can be a child or a parent, but the result is the same: The other family members are not encouraged or even permitted to express their own feelings or opinions. You will need to carefully monitor your sharing times to be sure all family members feel free to openly share what they are thinking and feeling.

Special Note for Parents: Listen well! When asked what they most want from adults, children invariably report that they want to be listened to. Many parents unknowingly close off communication with their children by talking too much. Giving your children full attention and affirming what they are telling you will work wonders in building relationships with them.

▶ **Family Rule #4: The unsolicited advice will be given.** A continuation of Rule #3, this rule is particularly important for parents whose communication style with their children tends to be one of lecturing or telling them what they should or should not do. Many parents see this as their primary role and do not realize that their well-intended instructions often closes off communication with their children. In your sharing times, encourage all family members to replace such confrontational statements are "*you* should" or If *you* would only" with "I" messages.

Of course, there will be times when you children do need guidance from you. If you sense that a child needs help, try giving permission to ask for it. "Would you like some help in thinking that through?" or "I'd be glad to help if you need help with that" is much more affirming to a child than "do it *my* way" messages. One word of caution: You must respect your child's right to say no to your offer of help. Hard as it may be to do, hold your advice until your child is ready to hear it.

▶ **Family Rule #5: It's okay to "pass."** It is important to let all members know they can be active participants and still have times when they do not feel ready to share their deepest thoughts and feelings. Sometimes opening up may feel painful or threatening, and at those times family members need to have the freedom to pass. An environment is not "friendly" or safe if people fear being pressured to talk about things they are not yet ready to share openly

▶ **Family Rule #6: It's okay to laugh and have fun together.** In today's high-stress world, many families have lost the ability to simply enjoy being with each other. Give your family permission to use the suggested activities as occasions to laugh, play, and make a mess together. You will find that much significant sharing and relationship building happens when family members are relaxed and enjoying one another's company.

There may be other family rules you would like to include for your family. Just remember that the purpose of each rule is to assure an environment that is safe, growth producing, and enjoyable for everyone!